Discerning The True Sentiments Of The Soul

The Revised and Enlarged Edition of the Booklet
Gauḍīya Vaiṣṇavism Versus Sahajiyāism

Discourses by
Śrī Śrīmad
Bhaktivedānta Nārāyaṇa Gosvāmī Mahārāja

GAUDIYA VEDANTA PUBLICATIONS
GVP

VRINDAVAN • NEW DELHI • SAN FRANCISCO

The printing of *Discerning the True Sentiments of the Soul* is financed by an endowment fund established by an anonymous donor and Jagannātha dāsa (Fiji), in memory of his good wife, Kṛṣṇa-līlā dāsī.

www.mygvp.com

Discerning the True Sentiments of the Soul

First edition 2014 – 3,000 copies
Printed in India at Samrat Offset Pvt. Ltd., Okhla Industrial Area, New Delhi

ISBN 978-1-935428-76-3
LCCN 2014930582

Cataloging in Publication Data--DK
Courtesy: D.K. Agencies (P) Ltd. <docinfo@dkagencies.com>

Bhaktivedānta Nārāyaṇa, 1921-
Discerning the true sentiments of the soul: the revised and enlarged edition of the booklet Gauḍīya Vaiṣṇavism versus Sahajiyāism / discourses by Bhaktivedānta Nārāyaṇa Gosvāmī Mahārāja. -- 1st ed.

p. cm.
Includes verses in Sanskrit (roman).
ISBN 9781935428763

1. Spiritual life--Chaitanya (Sect) I. Title.

DDC 294.544 23

Contents

Preface

Discerning the True Sentiments of the Soul is a revised and enlarged edition of the booklet *Gauḍīya Vaiṣṇavism Versus Sahajiyāism*, published in 1999. At that time our Śrīla Gurudeva, Śrī Śrīmad Bhaktivedānta Nārāyaṇa Gosvāmī Mahārāja, had given only the first two of these discourses in the West. Years later he gave related discourses, and we have added them to this publication in order to complete his exposition of this matter. We also listened again to the audio recordings of the original two lectures and collaborated to make some editorial revisions.

In these discourses, Śrīla Gurudeva quoted many Sanskrit and Bengali verses. We have included their translations in brackets within the text. The translations are either by Śrīla Gurudeva or by our most revered Śrīla Bhaktivedānta Svāmī Mahārāja, who is famous throughout the world as Śrīla Prabhupāda, and who is Śrīla Gurudeva's *śikṣā-guru* and close friend. An asterisk at the end of a translation indicates that it was done by Śrīla Prabhupāda.

Following the tradition of our spiritual preceptors, we use standard diacritical markings to indicate the pronunciation of the Sanskrit words. Pronounce **ā** like a in f**a**ther, **ī** like ea in n**ea**t, **ū** like oo in r**oo**t, **ṛ** like ri in **ri**p, **ṁ** and **ṇ** like ng in hu**ng**, **ś** and **ṣ** like sh in **sh**y, and **c** like ch in **ch**ap.

In a few places, in order to further explain or establish certain points of *siddhānta* given in Śrīla Gurudeva's lectures, we have also included quotes from Śrīla Prabhupāda's Vedabase folio within the endnotes and appendix. You will be happy to note that there is also an abbreviated glossary of Sanskrit terms at the back of the book.

While compiling these discourses, we asked Śrīla Gurudeva, as well as his secretary, Śrīpāda B. V. Mādhava Mahārāja, several questions in order to clarify some of the statements, and we have adjusted the body text accordingly.

It is only natural that since these lectures were given to different audiences in different places in different years, there was sometimes repetition of the same points. On a few occasions, while we were preparing some of Śrīla Gurudeva's lectures for publications on other themes, he had told us to remove instances of undue repetition. We have therefore followed his directive in this compilation.

Part I was spoken on June 27, 1997 at the ISKCON New Māyāpura farm community in France; Part II in Holland in the same year, on the auspicious Disappearance Day of Śrīla Bhaktivinoda Ṭhākura and Śrīla Gadādhara Paṇḍita; Part III on April 28, 1998, also in France; Part IV on June 10, 2001 in Holland; Part V in Murwillumbah, Australia, on December 3, 2002; and Part VI is comprised of two discourses given in Volgograd, Russia, on September 13, 2004 – *Why Not Only One Book?* is an excerpt from the morning discourse on that day, and *No Part to Disregard* is from the evening discourse.

Finally, Part VII consists of excerpts from Śrīla Gurudeva's biography of his own *dīkṣā-guru* and beloved life and soul, Śrī Śrīmad Bhakti Prajñāna Keśava Gosvāmī Mahārāja. In those sections of the biography, out of his immense compassion for sincere souls, Śrīla Gurudeva further elucidates the topic of true and false spiritual perfection.

Because he uttered an auspicious invocation at the beginning of each of his discourses in order to invoke blessings upon his audiences, we have included those prayers at the beginning of this book. We pray that you, our respected readers, will receive spiritual nourishment by reading these discourses.

Despite our best efforts, we may make some mistakes in presenting Śrīla Gurudeva's words. We invite you to assist in correcting any errors for the next print run. You can submit what you deem to be an error at www.purebhakti.com/gvp.

Praying for the service of Hari, Guru, and Vaiṣṇavas,
The publishing team
of *Discerning the True Sentiments of the Soul*

The Appearance Day of
Śrī Śrīmad Bhaktivedānta Nārāyaṇa Gosvāmī Mahārāja
January 30, 2014

Editorial Consultants – B. V. Mādhava Mahārāja, B. V. Tridaṇḍi Mahārāja, B. V. Vaikhānasa Mahārāja, Dāmodara dāsa (Toronto), Sulatā dāsī, Vaijayantī-mālā dāsī • **Editors** – Brajanāth dāsa, Sudevī dāsī (Malaysia), Śyāmārāṇī dāsī • **Transcriptions** – Devānanda dāsa, Madana-mohinī dāsī (Australia), Vasanti dāsī • **Corrections Typist** – Lalita-kiśorī dāsī • **Sound files** – Īśa dāsa of Purebhakti.tv • **Sound file fidelity check** – Tulasikā dāsī • **Glossary** – Sulatā dāsī • **Layout** – Jānakī dāsī • **Reader input** – Govinda dāsa, Ratikalā dāsī, Vasanti dāsī • **Proofreading** – Dāmodara dāsa, Jānakī dāsī, Sanātana dāsa • **Cover Design** – Ananta dāsa, Jayadeva dāsa, Kṛṣṇa-kāruṇya dāsa, Rādhā-mohana dāsa, Vasanta dāsa, Vijaya-kṛṣṇa dāsa (Manila) • **Front cover art** – Vāsudeva dāsa • **Technical Assistant** – Navalatikā dāsī • **Production coordinator** – Śyāmārāṇī dāsī • **Acknowledgements** – Alexander Muir, Ānandinī dāsī (U. K.), Ānitā dāsī, Jaya-gopāla dāsa, Kṛṣṇamayī dāsī, Mañjarī dāsī (Hawaii), Nṛsiṁha dāsa, Rāghava Paṇḍita dāsa, Śivānanda Sena dāsa, Yamunā dāsī

Śrī Śrīmad
Bhaktivedānta Nārāyaṇa Gosvāmī Mahārāja

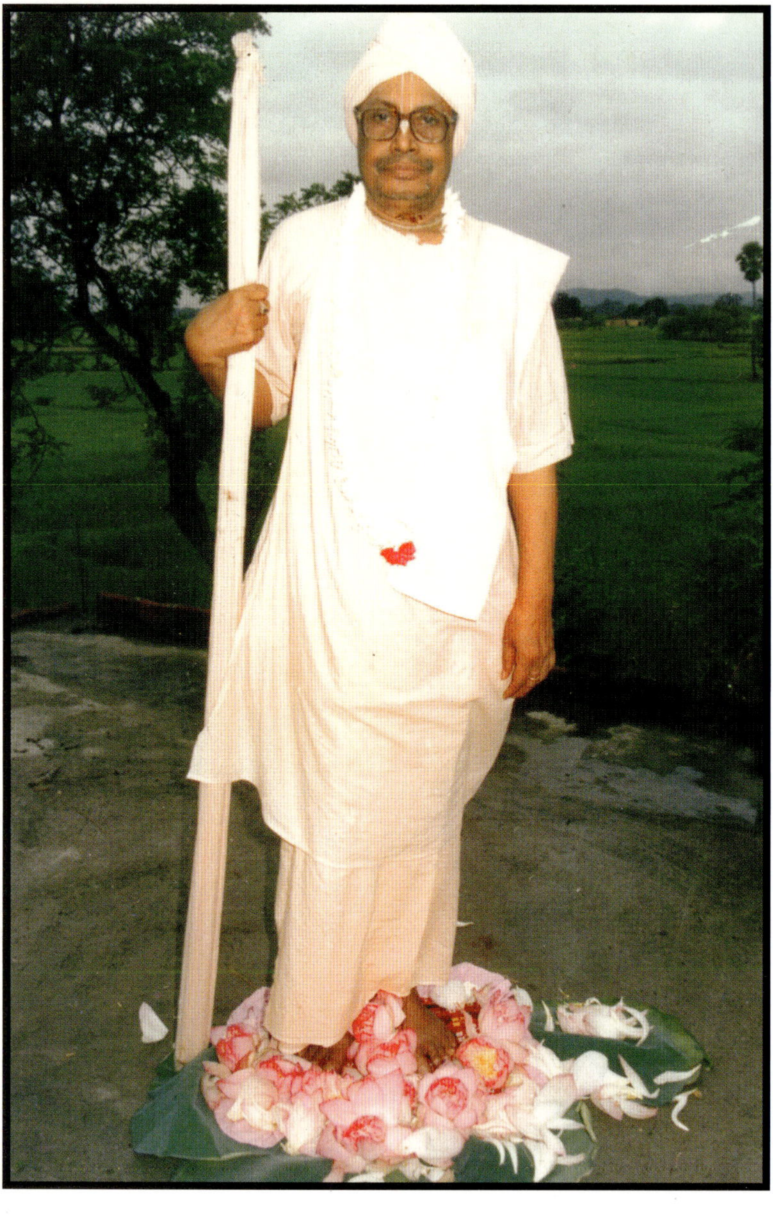

Śrī Śrīmad
Bhaktivedānta Vāmana Gosvāmī Mahārāja

Śrī Śrīmad
Bhaktivedānta Svāmī Mahārāja

Śrī Śrīmad
Bhakti Prajñāna Keśava Gosvāmī Mahārāja

Śrī Śrīmad
Bhaktisiddhānta Sarasvatī Ṭhākura Prabhupāda

Saccidānanda
Śrīla Bhaktivinoda Ṭhākura

Śrī Caitanya Mahāprabhu as
Śrī Śacīnandana Gaurahari

Śrī Kṛṣṇa, the Personality of Godhead, along with His supreme potency and beloved consort, Śrīmatī Rādhikā

An Introduction

First, we offer our unlimited obeisances to our most worshipful Gurudeva, *nitya-līlā praviṣṭa oṁ viṣṇupāda* Śrī Śrīmad Bhaktivedānta Nārāyaṇa Gosvāmī Mahārāja. For the spiritual upliftment of all souls in this world, he traveled the globe over thirty times, teaching the path of spiritual perfection – the practice of pure *bhakti-yoga*. We feel greatly honored to present herein a few of his discourses, which illuminate key elements of that practice.

These discourses clarify this bona fide path of the awakening of the full potential of the soul in a loving relationship with the Supreme Soul, Śrī Kṛṣṇa. Removal of obstructions on the path of that immaculate divine love by the causeless mercy of Śrī Guru opens the heart and allows that love to enter there. With this in mind, Śrīla Gurudeva also discussed those conceptions that are unfavorable for spiritual evolution. In particular, he focused on what he described as the widely spreading disease of *sahajiyāism*, a cheap imitation of spiritual realization that robs its followers of their true spiritual welfare.

For many of you, *Discerning the True Sentiments of the Soul* is your first book on *bhakti*, or one of your first. For your ease of understanding, we have defined two important terms that serve as the essential basis of its contents, namely Gauḍīya Vaiṣṇavism and *sahajiyāism*.

Gauḍīya Vaiṣṇavism

Vaiṣṇava refers to a devotee of Viṣṇu, the Supreme Personality of Godhead. There are innumerable Viṣṇu incarnations, and They appear regularly throughout history to display extraordinary pastimes. By witnessing or hearing about Their magnanimous activities, conditioned souls of this world become attracted; thus their natural quality, to engage in loving service (*bhakti*) to Visnu is awakened.

The Vedic scriptures state that the original Viṣṇu is Śrī Kṛṣṇa. They glorify Him as the source of all incarnations and all material and spiritual worlds, and as the Supreme Absolute Truth. This same Kṛṣṇa appeared on Earth 5,000 years ago, and His activities and teachings are recorded in the Vedic histories.

The Vedic literatures celebrate the Absolute Divinity together with His eternal feminine counterpart. Śrī Kṛṣṇa is the supreme transcendental male, and the supreme transcendental female is His loving consort, Śrīmatī Rādhikā. As Kṛṣṇa is the source of all Viṣṇu incarnations, Rādhikā is the source of all forms representing the female energy and creative potency (*śakti*), such as Lakṣmī, Pārvatī, Durgā, Sarasvatī, and Bhūmi, the Goddess of the Earth.

Rādhikā and Kṛṣṇa are One Truth, but They have separated Themselves into two eternal forms for the purpose of experiencing the highest form of loving pastimes together. In order to offer Kṛṣṇa the exultation of supreme bliss, Rādhikā serves Him in the mood of a paramour. Their exchanges appear similar to worldly relations between men and women, but careful analysis by self-realized souls reveals that they are completely devoid of material sentiment. The writings of the greatest sages and mystics, who themselves have no connection with worldly activities or attachments, extol the worship of Kṛṣṇa by Rādhikā and Her expansions, the *gopīs*, as the most exalted and purest form of love of God.

In the transcendental realm, Kṛṣṇa is the object of love and service, and Rādhikā and all devotees are the divine abode or vessel of that love. Both enjoy unlimited pleasure, yet Kṛṣṇa observes in Rādhikā the highest ecstatic love, the depths of which even He cannot fathom. Her love has qualities and pleasures that are not obtainable by Him as the object of love. Therefore, in order to understand the greatness of Her love, the happiness She feels in that love, and the unlimited magnificent qualities in Him that She alone relishes to the greatest extent, Śrī Kṛṣṇa covers Himself with Her mood and complexion and assumes a divine form known as Śrī Caitanya Mahāprabhu. Mahāprabhu appeared in this world more than five hundred years ago in the land of Gauḍa (present-day West Bengal), and those who follow Him and His teachings are called Gauḍīyas, or Gauḍīya Vaiṣṇavas.

Śrī Caitanya Mahāprabhu's appearance dissipates the darkness of ignorance enveloping this world. He delineated the basic precepts of pure *bhakti* and introduced the practice of *kīrtana*, the congregational chanting of the holy names of Śrī Kṛṣṇa, as the principle means to attain the super-excellence of that pure *bhakti*. He demonstrated the pristine perfection of the love of Śrī Rādhā and the *gopīs* for Kṛṣṇa, and, especially, He bestowed upon all fortunate souls the opportunity to attain direct service of Śrī Rādhā-Kṛṣṇa as a *gopī* maidservant by revealing through His authentic followers the process to achieve that.

The following is a brief summary of some of Mahāprabhu's teachings that have special relevance to *Discerning the True Sentiments of the Soul*. This summary is based on Śrīla Gurudeva's translation of and commentary on Śrīla Bhaktivinoda Ṭhākura's *Śrī Bhajana-rahasya* (Chapter 6, Text 6):

When the living entity, or *jīva*, is situated in his spiritual body (*siddha-deha*), his sole absorption is to lovingly serve Śrī Kṛṣṇa, and he deems his material designations insignificant.

By nature and constitution, the living entity is a servant of the transcendental Śrī Kṛṣṇa, the ocean of all nectarean mellows. This is confirmed in *Śrī Caitanya-caritāmṛta* (*Ādi-līlā* 5.142): Śrī Kṛṣṇa alone is Īśvara, the supreme controller, and all others are His servants. They dance as He makes them do so.

When the living entity is bound by the material energy (*māyā*), he identifies with the temporary material body as a woman, man or some other designation. Śrī Caitanya Mahāprabhu informed the human beings tormented by this iron age of Kali that they are not bound by social classes, such as *brāhmaṇas* (priests or teachers), *kṣatriyas* (soldiers or administrators), *vaiśyas* (businessmen or agriculturalists), or *sūdras* (laborers, technicians, or craftsmen), nor by the stages of life (householder, renunciant, etc.). Their pure, blissful identity is that of a loving servant of the servant of the servant of Śrī Kṛṣṇa, the Hero of the damsels of Vraja, the *gopīs*.

The destination a person attains after death is in accordance with his activities, impressions, and desires. But when he takes shelter of a bona fide *guru* and follows his instructions, he realizes his own eternal, pure form. By his dedication to serving his *guru* and chanting the holy name under his *guru's* guidance, his material identification is removed and a pure spiritual mood manifests. He then attains a transcendental body with which he can personally serve Kṛṣṇa.

One's transcendental body corresponds with one's mood of service, either as a servant, friend, parent, or beloved, and all such relationships are completely devoid of any desire for one's own happiness. A person who is inclined towards that rare love expressed by Rādhikā and the *gopīs* (*mādhurya-rasa*) will practice *bhakti* under the guidance of an authentic Vaiṣṇava and will attain a spiritual form that corresponds to this mood. This is the goal of the *rūpānuga* Gauḍīya Vaiṣṇavas.

Sahajiyāism

Throughout *Discerning the True Sentiments of the Soul*, Śrīla Gurudeva also discusses what the classical Vedic texts describe as the perverted reflection of this divine philosophy. He states that there is a dark reflection known as *sahajiyāism*, that its adherents are called *sahajiyās*, and that some *sahajiyā* groups are known as the *sahajiyā-bābājīs*. He explains that the moods of the *gopīs* are fully spiritual and are the nature of the most fortunate souls. In contrast, the *sahajiyās* in general, and *sahajiyā-bābājīs* specifically, think that it is possible to experience these spiritual emotions by imitating the spiritual activities of Rādhikā and Kṛṣṇa with one's material body and mind.

It may be noted here that Śrīla Gurudeva always acted and spoke with sincere affection for the welfare of all. Since clarity and discernment are essential for substantial spiritual progress, for which he was the most expert guide, he could not tolerate any adulteration of the words of scripture, as such adulteration is an impediment to pure *bhakti*. As a guardian of *bhakti*, if he saw persons about to do something to impede their spiritual progress, he would speak to them firmly, just like a loving parent. This would transform their hearts and inspire them to become deeply inclined to spiritual life. This is the miracle a real *guru* performs and this is his actual duty, nothing less.

In this book, Śrīla Gurudeva uses evidence from various Vedic texts to show the difference between mundane lust and spiritual love. He states, "Those who think that *parakīya-bhāva* (paramour love) is material, Kṛṣṇa is material, *bhakti* is material, and that we are this material body, have no conception of true, transcendental love nor *parakīya-bhāva*. They smoke *gāñjā* (marijuana). They desire to enjoy with many unmarried '*parakīya*' ladies, and these ladies also want many '*parakīya*' lovers, thus they all meet together and engage in all varieties of immoral behavior. Such persons will not be able to touch *bhakti* in millions upon millions of births; not even a semblance of *bhakti*."

Śrīla Gurudeva appeals to his audiences to take care regarding the *sahajiyās*: "We are preaching and therefore they are somewhat stopped, but I do now know what will happen after I leave this world. A very dangerous stage is coming." [1]

He explains that some male *sahajiyās* even dress and decorate themselves in the costumes of the *gopī* damsels and engage their so-called *gopī* followers in immoral escapades. Although males, they consider themselves to be Śrīmatī Rādhikā's eternal *sakhīs* (friends) and direct expansions, such as Lalitā, Viśākhā, or Rūpa Mañjarī. Because it is not possible for a living entity to become God or His direct expansions, this depraved misconception is akin to the *ahaṅgrahopāsanā* of the *māyāvādīs* (a type of worship in which one considers himself to be identical with the object of worship).

He explains that some groups of *sahajiyās* give pretentious lectures on and try to imitate *rāsa-līlā*, Kṛṣṇa's divine dance with the *gopīs*. Some, calling themselves Gauḍīya Vaiṣṇavas and at the same time acting immorally, have inspired the educated and respectable members of society to despise the very name 'Gauḍīya Vaiṣṇava.' Some are highly critical of the self-realized souls in the line of Śrī Caitanya Mahāprabhu, who are truly propagating His sublime message. And some, although in various ways acting as genuine Gauḍīya Vaiṣṇavas and even

1 Excerpt from Śrīla Bhaktivedānta Nārāyaṇa Gosvāmī Mahārāja's morning discouse in Olpe, Germany, on February 21, 2003.

associating with pure devotees, meet in seclusion with those of the opposite gender to discuss with a mundane mood the confidential pastimes of Śrī Rādhā and Kṛṣṇa.

Not all varieties of materialistic philosophical amalgamations are specifically discussed by Śrīla Gurudeva in *Discerning the True Sentiments of the Soul*, although they are mentioned in some of his other books. Still, a careful reader will be able to utilize his words to recognize other philosophies opposed to pure *bhakti*. Both in the East and West, where *yoga*, *kīrtana*, *bhakti*, *dharma*, *karma*, and *guru* are practically household words, such speculative malpractices and opinions include: "I am God, you are God, we are all one with that impersonal God in all respects;" "God is Zero;" "There are many Gods;" "Service to man is service to God;" "All paths lead to the same destination;" "Consciousness comes from matter;" "We are proud that our God is Kṛṣṇa, because He freely sported with women and our spiritual perfection is to do the same;" etc.

Following in the footsteps of his disciplic predecessors in the line of Śrī Caitanya Mahāprabhu, our most revered holy master Śrīla Bhaktivedānta Nārāyaṇa Gosvāmī Mahārāja has established the dignity and greatness of true Gauḍīya Vaiṣṇava culture by his books, discourses, conversations, and sacred presence. We pray at his lotus feet that he sprinkle his causeless mercy upon us, to bestow upon us the spiritual intelligence to always discern the true and blissful sentiments of the ever-pure soul.

Your aspiring servants,
The editors

Auspicious Invocation

oṁ ajñāna-timirāndhasya jñānāñjana-śalākayā
cakṣur unmīlitaṁ yena tasmai śrī-gurave nāmaḥ

(*Śrī Guru praṇāma*)

O Gurudeva, you are so merciful. I offer my humble *praṇāma* to you and am praying from the core of my heart that with the torchlight of divine knowledge you open my eyes, which have been blinded by the darkness of ignorance.

vāñchā-kalpa-tarubyaś ca kṛpā-sindhubhya eva ca
patitānāṁ pāvanebhyo vaiṣṇavebhyo namo nāmaḥ

(*Śrī Vaiṣṇava vandanā*)

I offer *praṇāma* unto the Vaiṣṇavas, who are just like wish-fulfilling desire trees, who are an ocean of mercy, and who deliver the fallen, conditioned souls.

namo mahā-vadānyāya kṛṣṇa-prema-pradāya te
kṛṣṇāya kṛṣṇa-caitanya-nāmne gaura-tviṣe nāmaḥ

(*Śrīman Mahāprabhu vandanā*)

I offer *praṇāma* unto Śrī Kṛṣṇa Caitanya, who is Śrī Kṛṣṇa Himself. Having assumed the golden hue of Śrīmatī Rādhikā, He is munificently bestowing *kṛṣṇa-prema* (pure love for Kṛṣṇa), the rarest of all gifts.

gurave gauracandrāya rādhikāyai tadālaye
kṛṣṇāya kṛṣṇa-bhaktāya tad-bhaktāya namo nāmaḥ

(*Samaṣṭigata praṇāma*)

I offer my obeisances time and again unto *śrī guru*, Śrī Gauracandra, Śrīmatī Rādhikā, Her associates and Her abode Śrī Vṛndāvana-dhāma, and unto Śrī Kṛṣṇa and all of His devotees.

bhaktyā vihīnā aparādha-lakṣaiḥ
kṣiptāś ca kāmādi-taraṅga-madhye
kṛpāmayi! tvāṁ śaraṇaṁ prapānnā
vṛnde! numas te caraṇāravindam

(*Śrī Vṛndā-devyaṣṭakam*, Verse 8)

Devoid of *bhakti* and guilty of unlimited offenses, we are flung into the waves of lust [anger, greed, and so on]. O merciful one, we take shelter of you! O Vṛndā, we offer *praṇāma* to your lotus feet.

yaṁ pravrajantam anupetam apeta-kṛtyaṁ
dvaipāyano viraha-kātara ājuhāva
putreti tan-mayatayā taravo 'bhinedus
taṁ sarva-bhūta-hṛdayaṁ munim ānato 'smi

(*Śrīmad-Bhāgavatam* 1.2.2)

I offer *praṇāma* to Śrī Śukadeva Gosvāmī, who can enter the hearts of all people. When he left home without undergoing the purificatory processes, such as accepting the sacred thread, his father Vyāsa cried out, "O my son!" As if they were absorbed in the same feelings of separation, the trees echoed in response to his call.

Part I

Real and Unreal Spiritual Body

A Boy's Imagination

Once, a very little boy of three or four years, sitting naked on the lap of his mother, put his arms around his mother's neck and said with love and affection, "Mother, Mother, I want a very beautiful wife. She should have a golden complexion, curly hair and beautiful eyes. She should not be stronger than me, otherwise she will be able to chastise me, and she should be thinner than me. Also, I want to have two sons and one daughter soon after our marriage. Quickly, Mother, please arrange for a very beautiful lady."

The boy's mother began to laugh. "Yes," she replied. "I will certainly search everywhere for a good wife for you, but first you must become bigger and stronger. Then, when your *śikhā*[1] becomes long and thick, I will quickly arrange your marriage."

This story indicates a phenomenon that is widely spreading among so-called devotees nowadays. Such persons hardly chant any rounds of Kṛṣṇa's holy names on their *japa* beads,

---

1 A lock of unshaved hair on the upper, back part of the head.

nor do they make an effort to develop a devotional mood towards Kṛṣṇa. They have no desire to remember Kṛṣṇa, nor do they want to enter into a deep understanding of *siddhānta*, or conclusive spiritual truths. They are not interested in chanting throughout the day and night like Śrīla Haridāsa Ṭhākura, and in fact they cannot even chant one round of the Hare Kṛṣṇa *mantra* with their minds absorbed in Kṛṣṇa. They have many requirements to think about for the body and for things that relate to the body, such as name, fame, and fortune. They are overcome by lust and other worldly desires – and yet they expect the manifestation of their *siddha-deha*, or perfected spiritual body by which a pure soul can render transcendental service unto Śrī Rādhikā and Kṛṣṇa.

Jumping Into Goloka

Although their minds cannot concentrate on Kṛṣṇa's transcendental pastimes, such persons want *siddha-deha* as if it were an Indian *rasagulla* (milk-sweet). If someone has money, he can easily purchase two, three, or four *rasagullas*. Similarly, these persons think that they can attain their spiritual body as easily as one buys a *rasagulla*, but their philosophical misconception has extremely dangerous consequences.

These neophytes expect to immediately jump into Goloka Vṛndāvana and serve Kṛṣṇa better than Śrīmatī Rādhikā, Śrī Kṛṣṇa's supreme potency and beloved consort. They proudly say, "Rādhikā? Who is this Rādhikā? Who is this Lalitā? Who is this Viśākhā?" At the same time, if a beautiful young lady or man were to come along, practicing her or his own false devotional life with similar misconceptions, the two would lustfully fall down together in a moment.

There are thousands upon thousands of such so-called devotees. Although not mature in their performance of devotional service (*bhakti*), they artificially think, "I have now achieved my *siddha-deha*; I am Lalitā, or Viśākhā, and I am a better maidservant than Rūpa Mañjarī. Rūpa Mañjarī is not as qualified as I am." As a result of this offensive thinking, such persons necessarily go to hell in a very short time – in a day or two.

These people also think, "Oh, the Gauḍīya Maṭha has deviated from the ancient *paramparā* (the disciplic succession of bona fide *ācāryas*, or spiritual masters). The previous *ācāryas* used to think and act like us. Rūpa Gosvāmī and all other *ācāryas* used to do as we do. From the beginning stage of their devotional lives they remembered their *siddha-deha*, and in that spiritual form they served Kṛṣṇa."

Such speculations are quite wrong. Our *ācāryas*, headed by the six Gosvāmīs, never acted like this. They are not ordinary persons. They are the personal associates of Śrī Śrī Rādhā and Kṛṣṇa, and they have descended to this world only to give their mercy and teachings. They set the example in their own lives for the conditioned souls by beginning from *śraddhā* – faith in the words of *guru*, *sādhu* (a highly-realized soul), and *śāstra* (Vedic scripture), and the firm conviction that all subsidiary activities are accomplished automatically by rendering loving service to Kṛṣṇa.

Siddha-deha, Our Spiritual Body

In his book *Jaiva-dharma*, Śrīla Bhaktivinoda Ṭhākura has described all the principles and practices of *bhakti* up to the attainment of one's *siddha-deha*. There he has explained the eleven items of perfection:

(1) *sambandha* (one's personal relationship with Śrī Śrī Rādhā and Kṛṣṇa)

(2) *vayasa* (the age of one's soul as a *gopī*, a young cowherd maiden of Vraja, in that personal relationship)

(3) *nāma* (the name of one's soul as a *gopī* in that personal relationship)
(4) *rūpa* (one's personal form and beauty)
(5) *yūtha* (the group in which one serves the Divine Couple)
(6) *veśa* (one's dress)
(7) *ājñā* (one's specific instruction)
(8) *vāsa* (one's residence in Goloka Vṛndāvana)
(9) *sevā* (one's exclusive service)
(10) *parākāṣṭhā-śvāsa* (the highest summit of emotion, which is the aspirant's very life-breath)
(11) *pālyadāsī-bhāva* (the sentiment of a maidservant under the protection of Śrī Rādhā)

But he discussed this in the last pages of *Jaiva-dharma*, not in the beginning. It is stated there that Śrī Raghunātha dāsa Bābājī[2] sent his disciple Vijaya-kumāra to Gopāla Guru Gosvāmī in Puri, so that Vijaya-kumāra could hear from him about these principles of perfection. However, that would be when Vijaya Kumāra would be advanced in Kṛṣṇa consciousness and free from all material desires and *anarthas* (impurities of the heart).

Vijaya-kumāra had been chanting and remembering Kṛṣṇa twenty-four hours a day on the shore of the ocean at Jagannātha Purī. In fact, the ocean always reminded him of Kṛṣṇa, the ocean of *rasa*, or transcendental mellows. Vijaya-kumāra had understood and realized the meaning of *vibhāva* (the two causes of relishing *prema*), *anubhāva* (the subordinate signs of ecstatic emotion, such as rolling on the ground and laughing loudly), *sāttvika* (the eight symptoms of constitutional ecstasy, such as perspiring, faltering of the voice, and trembling), and *vyābhicārī* (the thirty-three ecstatic symptoms that are like waves in the

2 In *Jaiva-dharma*, the word '*bābājī*' does not refer to the *sahajiyā bābājīs*. This address or title is part of the general custom within Vedic culture. '*Bābā*' refers to an elderly, senior person, and '*jī*' is an address of affection and respect.

nectar ocean of *sthāyībhāva*, one's eternal relationship with Kṛṣṇa, which rise from and then again disappear into that ocean).[3]

Vijaya-kumāra also realized in what proportion these ingredients would need to be mixed with one's *sthāyībhāva* in order to become *bhakti-rasa*, the mellow exchanges in love for Kṛṣṇa. As he was on the stage of *bhāva-bhakti*, transcendental emotion, he had become truly humble.

tṛṇād api sunīcena taror api sahiṣṇunā
amāninā māna-dena kīrtanīyaḥ sadā hariḥ

(*Śikṣāṣṭaka* 3)

[Thinking oneself to be even lower and more worthless than insignificant grass that has been trampled beneath everyone's feet, being more tolerant than a tree, being prideless, and offering respect to all others according to their respective positions, one should continuously chant the holy name of Śrī Hari.]

Menaka and other Apsarās, celestial goddesses, who are more beautiful than any earthly women, cannot disturb the Kṛṣṇa consciousness of a person like Śrīla Haridāsa Ṭhākura. Yet, even Śrīla Haridāsa Ṭhākura was not engaged in the advanced practices of devotees in the Gosvāmī line such as Vijaya-kumāra. We have never seen or heard in any scriptures that he was engaged in this way. Only devotees like Śrīla Rūpa Gosvāmī, Śrīla Sanātana Gosvāmī, and Śrīla Raghunātha dāsa Gosvāmīs were following all of these principles, and our entire line of disciplic succession has continued in the same way down to the present day.

A devotee must become mature in *bhakti* before he is able to fully comprehend the *ācāryas* in our disciplic line. He must

3 See Endnote 1, at the end of this chapter.

come to the stage of *śraddhā*, the firm faith that simply by the performance of devotional service to Śrī Kṛṣṇa, all subsidiary activities are automatically performed. He then comes to *sādhu-saṅga*, the association of pure devotees, and in that association he engages in *bhajana-kriyā*, the execution of *bhakti* practices. By such execution he gradually comes to the stage of *anartha-nivṛtti*, freedom from habits and thoughts that are unfavorable to *bhakti*, then *niṣṭhā*, or steadiness, then *ruci*, taste in chanting and other devotional practices, and then *āsakti*, natural attachment to Kṛṣṇa. After that, at the stage of *bhāva*, when there is no longer a scent of desire for sense gratification, when he is quite free from all material thoughts and habits, his *siddha-deha*, or constitutional form, automatically manifests.

The Eight Stages of Spiritual Advancement

When will *siddha-deha* manifest? Śrīla Bhaktivinoda Ṭhākura has discussed this in his book *Bhajana-rahasya*. There he explains Śrī Caitanya Mahāprabhu's *Śikṣāṣṭaka*, which illuminates the eight stages of maturity in devotional service. He writes that one will first have to do *bhajana*, internal absorption and external practice, of *ceto-darpaṇa-mārjanaṁ*:

ceto-darpaṇa-mārjanaṁ bhava-mahā-dāvāgni-nirvāpaṇaṁ
śreyaḥ-kairava-candrikā-vitaraṇaṁ vidyā-vadhū-jīvanam
ānandāmbudhi-vardhanaṁ prati-padaṁ pūrṇāmṛtāsvādanaṁ
sarvātma-snapānaṁ paraṁ vijayate śrī-kṛṣṇa-saṅkīrtanaṁ

(*Śikṣāṣṭaka* 1)

[Let there be supreme victory for the chanting of the holy name of Śrī Kṛṣṇa, which cleanses the mirror of the heart and completely extinguishes the blazing forest fire of material existence. *Śrī-kṛṣṇa-saṅkīrtana* diffuses the soothing moon rays of *bhāva*, which cause the white lotus of good fortune for the living entities to bloom.

The holy name is the life and soul of transcendental knowledge, which is here compared to a consort (*vadhū*). It continuously expands the ocean of transcendental bliss, enabling one to taste complete nectar at every step. The holy name of Śrī Kṛṣṇa thoroughly cleanses and cools one's self (*ātmā*), one's nature, one's determination, and one's body, both internally and externally.]

This verse of *Śrī Śikṣāṣṭaka* is actually realized after reaching the stage of *āsakti*, or natural attachment for Śrī Śrī Rādhikā and Kṛṣṇa.

Then, the second verse:

nāmnām akāri bahudhā nija-sarva-śaktis
tatrārpitā niyamitaḥ smaraṇe na kālaḥ
etādṛśī tava kṛpā bhagavan mamāpi
durdaivam īdṛśam ihājani nānurāgaḥ

[O Lord! Your holy name bestows all auspiciousness upon the living entities. Therefore, for their benefit, You eternally manifest Your innumerable names, such as Rāma, Nārāyaṇa, Kṛṣṇa, Mukuṇḍa, Mādhava, Govinda, Dāmodara, and so on. You have invested those names with all the potencies of Your various personal forms.

Out of causeless mercy, You have not imposed any restrictions on the chanting and remembrance of such names in regard to any specified time, such as *sandhyā-vandanā* (evening prayer). In other words, at any time of the day or night, the holy name can be chanted and remembered. This is the concession You have granted.

O Lord! On account of committing offenses (*nāma-aparādha*), I am so unfortunate that although Your Holy name is so easily accessible and bestows all good fortune, no attachment has awoken in me for chanting.]

This verse represents the stages of *sādhu-saṅga* (the association of highly advanced devotees), and *anartha-nivṛtti*; that is, the removal of unwanted habits and thoughts by such association. At present, our chanting of Kṛṣṇa's name is not pure;[4] it may sometimes be *nāmābhāsa*, which is the clearing stage of chanting, or *nāma-aparādha*, chanting with ten offenses.[5]

Pure *nāma* will appear on our tongue when we become pure ourselves. At that time the qualities of humility and forbearance, as given in the third verse, will automatically manifest.

tṛṇādapi sunīcena
taror api sahiṣṇunā
amāninā mānadena
kīrtanīyaḥ sadā hariḥ

[Thinking oneself to be even lower and more worthless than insignificant grass that has been trampled beneath everyone's feet, being more tolerant than a tree, being prideless, and offering respect to all others according to their respective positions, one should continuously chant the holy name of Śrī Hari.]

---

4 "There is one word by Śrīla Bhaktivinoda Ṭhākura: '*nāmākṣara bahir haya nāma nāhi haya* – simply the alphabets are coming, but that is not *nāma.*' *Nāmākṣara*, Hare Kṛṣṇa, the alphabets, are coming out, but it is not the holy name" (Śrīla Bhaktivedānta Svāmī Prabhupāda in a room conversation, Māyāpura, February 25, 1977).

5 See Endnote 2, at the end of this chapter.

Now the forth verse:

na dhanaṁ na janaṁ na sundarīṁ
kavitāṁ vā jagadīśa kāmaye
mama janmani janmanīśvare
bhavatād bhaktir ahaitukī tvayi

[O Jagadīśa, Lord of the universe! I do not desire wealth, followers such as wife, sons, and relatives, or mundane knowledge described in poetic language. My only desire, O Lord of my life, is that birth after birth I may have causeless devotional service unto Your lotus feet.]

This fourth verse represents *ruci*, or taste, for *bhajana*. When we properly practice *bhajana* in good association, everything will develop automatically. We will then realize the fifth *śloka*, which represents *āsakti*. It is at this stage that one's *siddha-deha* begins to manifest:

ayi nanda-tanuja kiṅkaraṁ
patitaṁ māṁ viṣame bhavāmbudhau
kṛpayā tava pāda-paṅkaja-
sthita-dhūli-sadṛśaṁ vicintaya

[O Nanda-nandana, O divine son of Nanda Mahārāja! Please be merciful upon me, Your eternal servant, who has fallen in the dreadful ocean of material existence as a result of my fruitive actions. Like a particle of dust affixed to Your lotus feet, kindly accept me forever as Your purchased servant.]

After the stage of *āsakti*, when the devotee's tears of ecstasy flow continuously, he feels *pūrva-rāga*, the intense mood of separation experienced before meeting Kṛṣṇa. As he chants, he thinks, "O Kṛṣṇa, I cannot live without You, O Śrīmatī Rādhikā,

I cannot live without You. When will You give me Your *darśana* (direct audience)?"

Then, when he is weeping twenty-four hours daily, rolling on the earth, he realizes *Śikṣāṣṭaka's* sixth verse:

nayanaṁ galad-aśru-dhārayā
vadanaṁ gadgada-ruddhayā girā
pulakair nicitaṁ vapuḥ kadā,
tava nāma-grahaṇe bhaviṣyati

[O Prabhu! When will my eyes be filled with a stream of tears? When will my voice choke up? And when will the hairs of my body stand erect in ecstasy as I chant Your holy names?]

This verse represents the stage of *bhāva*, at which time one's *siddha-deha* manifests naturally. From where does it come? It is in our *svarūpa*, our original spiritual form. It does not come from anywhere outside ourselves. Everything is perfect in our constitutional spiritual form, and to realize this we simply require a connection with *svarūpa-śakti*, the Lord's internal potency.[6] When that connection is made, our perfect spiritual form automatically manifests and all the spiritual sentiments of love appear in our heart.

Kṛṣṇa Will Arrange Everything

Kṛṣṇa will arrange everything. A person need not become mad and artificially imitate this stage, otherwise he will find himself outside this spiritual Gauḍīya Vaiṣṇava line. It is essential to long for the day when our *siddha-deha* will appear, but not to imagine that we have attained it before it has actually manifested. We can only pray, "O Kṛṣṇa, I want to be eternally in Vṛndāvana, in a transcendental body. O Kṛṣṇa! O Gurudeva!

6 See Endnote 3, at the end of this chapter.

When will I have *siddha-deha* and *siddha-nāma*, the name of my pure soul? O Śrīmatī Rādhikā! When will I become Your maidservant, Your *pālya-dāsī*? When will I reside with You near Govardhana and Rādhā-kuṇḍa? When will I attain that position?"

We should always have that as our objective, hankering to attain service to Rādhā and Kṛṣṇa, but not imagining that we are Śrīmatī Rādhikā's intimate *sakhīs*[7], devoted friends, like Lalitā, Viśākhā, or any other *sakhī*, otherwise we will be ruined.

Patience is required. In the First Canto of *Śrīmad-Bhāgavatam* it is stated that Śrī Nārada Muni had been meditating and performing austerities for many years in order to realize the Lord. After that, Lord Nārāyaṇa appeared to him for a moment and then disappeared. Śrī Nārada immediately became upset and lamented, "Oh, Lord Nārāyaṇa has gone. What shall I do?" When he began to weep loudly, a voice called to him from the sky, assuring him, "Don't worry. You will have to wait, because no one can see Me in his material body. By My mercy I showed you My form for a moment, but now you must wait. Continue chanting My names and remembering Me twenty-four hours daily wherever you are, and preach My *hari-kathā* (narrations of Śrī Hari and His associates) to others. One day death will come, at which time you will put your feet on its head and quickly give up your material body."

prayujyamāne mayi tāṁ
śuddhāṁ bhāgavatīṁ tanum
ārabdha-karma-nirvāṇo
nyapatat pāñca-bhautikaḥ

(*Śrīmad-Bhāgavatam* 1.6.28)

---

7 The word *sakhī* refers, in general, to a teenage *gopī* (cowherd damsel), an elderly *gopī*, a maidservant of Śrīmatī Rādhikā, or to any friend of Rādhikā, depending on the context –Ed.

> [Having been awarded a transcendental body befitting an associate of the Personality of Godhead, I quit the body made of five material elements, and thus all acquired fruitive results of work (*karma*) stopped.*]

At the time of death, when Śrī Nārada Muni left his body made of five material elements, his *siddha-deha* appeared and he realized himself as an associate of the Supreme Lord. When did this perfection come? Not in the beginning. It came at the most advanced stage of his Kṛṣṇa consciousness.

We can expect to attain our *siddha-deha* when we have understood all *siddhānta*, conclusive spiritual truths. One who does not care to know such truths will say, "This fire (the activities of artificial spiritual perfection) is my *mahā-prasāda* (remnants of food or other articles offered to the Deity)." In other words, that person will accept his misconception as the Lord's remnants, or the Lord's mercy. He will eat that fire and be finished.

This misconception is called *sahajiyāism*,[8] and there is a great difference between *sahajiyās* and real Gauḍīya Vaiṣṇavas.[9] Śrīla Rūpa Gosvāmī and Śrīla Sanātana Gosvāmī were not *sahajiyās*. They were actually following the correct process of *bhakti*.

The word *siddha* indicates that a person must first become a *siddha*, perfect, devotee. In our Gosvāmīs' books, especially in the books of Śrīla Rūpa Gosvāmī and Śrīla Raghunātha dāsa Gosvāmī, the bona fide process for achieving perfection is explicitly given. The aspiring devotee first understands Prahlāda Mahārāja in the Seventh Canto of *Śrīmad-Bhāgavatam* and then Citraketu Mahārāja in the Sixth Canto. Then he understands the first part of Tenth Canto, especially how Kṛṣṇa manifested His

---

8 See Endnote 4, at the end of this chapter.

9 Please see pages vi–x of the Introduction for an elaborate definition of *sahajiyāism* and Gauḍīya Vaiṣṇavism.

dāmodara-līlā, His pastimes as a young child, and he remembers all these pastimes. His devotion must mature, so that seeing a beautiful young lady or man will not disturb him or her. He comes to the stage in which he has no worldly desires at all, and he is qualified to remain in Vṛndāvana and Rādhā-kuṇḍa under the guidance of a self-realized soul who knows all established philosophical truths (*tattvā-jña*) and is relishing the mellows of devotion (*rasika bhakta*).

Spreading Like a Plague

There are so many *sahajiyā bābājīs* – men and women – in Rādhā-kuṇḍa, Vṛndāvana, Kāmyavana, and other areas in Vraja. Coming to Govardhana and Mathurā to beg money in the shops and other places, and then spending the entire night counting the money they collected, how will they have time to chant and remember Kṛṣṇa and to practice *bhakti*? They say that their *guru* gave them *siddha-deha*, and at the same time they don't even know how to clean themselves after passing stool and urine. Thoroughly bereft of even the ABCs of *siddhānta*, they imagine that they have been given perfection.

Not only in India, but also throughout the world, there is a lack of understanding and good association, which has created a serious plague that is spreading like wildfire among neophyte devotees. We must try to save ourselves from this. Nowadays, even brand new devotees are reading *Kṛṣṇa-bhāvanāmṛta* and saying, "Oh, very good, very good." They are reading *Govinda-līlāmṛta* and thinking, "Oh, this is wonderful! The Gauḍīya Maṭha does not know all these things. They cannot taste *rasa* (transcendental mellows), whereas we are submerged in *rasa*."

Instead of following this perilous path, the sincere spiritual aspirant tries to pursue the bona fide process laid down by *ācāryas* like Śrīla Bhaktivinoda Ṭhākura. At our present neophyte stage it is not favorable to buy or read *Govinda-līlāmṛta*, *Kṛṣṇa-bhāvanāmṛta*, *Muktā-carita*, *Dāna-keli-cintāmaṇi*, or *Dāna-keli-kaumudī*. Let us first engage in very good *sādhana-bhajana* and become mature in *bhakti*. Until then, we don't need to read these books any more than the three-year-old boy required a beautiful wife. Let us not be involved in that dream.

If we follow sincerely, Kṛṣṇa will automatically send a realized soul to help us. He may send Śrīla Bhaktivinoda Ṭhākura, or Śrīla Rūpa Gosvāmī may come. Or, Śrī Caitanya Mahāprabhu may personally come in some form.

Our Aim and Objective

If we know the aim and objective of our *sādhana*, we can then begin from *śraddhā*. These are the steps:

ādau śraddhā tataḥ sādhu-saṅgo 'tha bhajana-kriyā
tato 'nartha-nivṛttiḥ syāt tato niṣṭhā rucis tataḥ
athāsaktis tato bhāvas tataḥ premābhyudañcati
sādhakānām ayaṁ premṇaḥ prādurbhāve bhavet kramaḥ

(*Bhakti-rasāmṛta-sindhu* 1.4.15–16)

[(1) Hearing the *śāstras*, or Vedic scriptures, gives rise to *pāramārthika śraddhā*, or firm belief in the meaning of the *bhakti-śāstras*, such as *Śrīmad Bhagavad-gītā*, *Śrīmad-Bhāgavatam*, *Bhakti-rasāmṛta-sindhu*, and so forth.

(2) Upon the appearance of such *śraddhā*, one again obtains *sādhu-saṅga* (association of pure devotees), and, in the company of *sādhus*, begins to receive instructions regarding the methods for executing *bhajana*.

(3) Thereafter, one engages in *bhajana-kriyā*, the practices of *bhajana*, beginning with taking shelter of a bona fide *guru* (*śrī-guru-padāśraya*) and so on.

(4) By constant engagement in *bhajana*, habits and thoughts that are unfavorable in the development of *bhakti* gradually disappear (*anartha-nivṛtti*).

(5) This elimination of *anarthas* takes place in successive stages. As one becomes progressively freed from *anarthas*, he attains *niṣṭhā*, steadiness in *bhakti* and freedom from all distractions. At that stage, one-pointedness and incessant striving arise in the pursuit of *bhajana*.

(6) Thereafter, *ruci* (taste), or, in other words, an intense hankering for *bhajana*, develops.

(7) When *ruci* becomes very deep it is called *āsakti*. The difference between *niṣṭhā* and *āsakti* is that *niṣṭhā* involves application of the intelligence, whereas *āsakti* is spontaneous. In the stage of *niṣṭhā*, even if the mind is not attracted, by one's intelligence one remains devoted to the performance of *bhajana*. However, when one comes to the stage of *āsakti*, the *sādhaka*, or devotional practitioner, has no more dependence on any kind of reasoning by the faculty of the intelligence. At that stage he is deeply immersed in the performance of *bhajana* in a spontaneous manner.

(8) After the stage of *āsakti*, genuine spiritual emotion (*bhāva*, or *rati*) makes its appearance.

(9) At the final stage, *prema*, pure love of Godhead, manifests. This is the order of the stages leading to the appearance of *prema* within the heart of the *sādhaka*.]

When you reach *bhāva-bhakti*, you will realize and practice this verse:

kṣāntir avyartha-kālatvaṁ
viraktir māna-śūnyatā
āśā-bandhaḥ samutkaṇṭhā
nāma-gāne sadā-ruciḥ

āsaktis tad-guṇākhyāne
prītis tad vasati-sthale
ity ādayo 'nubhāvāḥ syur
jāta-bhāvāṅkure jane
(*Bhakti-rasāmṛta-sindhu* 1.3.25–26)

[When the seed of ecstatic emotion for Kṛṣṇa fructifies, the following nine symptoms manifest in one's behavior: forgiveness (*kṣānti*), concern that time should not be wasted (*avyartha-kālatva*), detachment (*virakti*), absence of false prestige (*māna-śūnyatā*), hope (*āśā-bandha*), eagerness (*samutkaṇṭhā*), a taste for chanting the holy name of the Lord (*nāma-gāne sadā-ruci*), attachment to descriptions of the transcendental qualities of the Lord (*tad-guṇākhyāne āsakti*), and affection for those places where the Lord resides (*tad-vasati-sthale prīti*) – that is, a temple or a holy place like Vṛndāvana. These are all called *anubhāvas*, subordinate signs of ecstatic emotion. They are visible in a person in whose heart the seed of love of God has begun to fructify.*]

By understanding all these truths we can adopt the correct process, but it is not that there are no devotees who are already qualified to remember their *siddha-deha*. There are certainly pure devotees in this world. They will not be disturbed by the *sahajiyās'* criticism, of course; rather those who criticize or imitate them will be disturbed. Such persons will not profit by trying to artificially drag such pure devotees down to their level. There may be thousands of devotees who are qualified for this perfection, and who are already perfect at the present moment.

One of the symptoms of a devotee who has achieved *bhāva-bhakti* is "*nāma-gāne sadā-ruci, laya kṛṣṇa-nāma* – Due to having great relish for the holy name, one is inclined to chant the Hare

Kṛṣṇa *mahā-mantra* constantly"* (*Śrī Caitanya-caritāmṛta, Madhya-līlā* 23.32). This devotee chants even in dreams, or sleep. He has so much taste for chanting that he cannot give it up at any time.

Do you know who is the best *kīrtaniyā* (the best performer of chanting Kṛṣṇa's names and glories) in the entire world from ancient times to the present day? Do you know who sings the most powerful and sweet *kīrtanas*? It is not necessarily the person who is expert at playing violin, harmonium, *tablā*, and *vīṇā*.

Śrīla Śukadeva Gosvāmī is the best *kīrtaniyā*. All our *ācāryas* are the best *kīrtaniyās*. Śrīla Bhaktivinoda Ṭhākura, Śrīla Bhaktisiddhānta Sarasvatī Gosvāmī Ṭhākura, and Śrīla Bhaktivedānta Svāmī Mahārāja are also the best *kīrtaniyās*.

Understand this deeply, and try to become *kīrtaniyās* like our *ācāryas*. There is no need to think yourself unqualified if you don't know how to play the harmonium or if your voice cannot sing *rāga-raginīs*. Even a raspy voice is no impediment. Simply chant with feeling, "Alas, Kṛṣṇa! Alas, Kṛṣṇa!"

It is the spiritual qualification to describe the pastimes of Kṛṣṇa that makes one the most high-class *kīrtaniyā*, not a fine voice. A person with a beautiful voice may fall down at any time, and in fact he may already be fallen. Those who perform *kīrtana* thinking, "Are the people in the audience inspired, or not? Are they pleased with my *kīrtana*?" are not actually doing *kīrtana*. *Kīrtana* is that process by which the transcendental sound of Kṛṣṇa's name and glories enters the ears and purifies the heart.

If we have to glorify a person, or if we have to give him rupees, dollars, or francs before he will sing, then he is not truly a *kīrtaniyā*. Money and reputation cannot touch the real *kīrtaniyā*. We want to be like that: melting others' hearts, melting our own hearts, and always weeping for Śrī Śrī Rādhā and Kṛṣṇa. The *hari-kathā* of such a *kīrtaniyā* touches everyone's hearts, and all sincere souls are bound to follow him. Such a person is *guru*.

vāco vegaṁ manasaḥ krodha-vegaṁ
jihvā-vegam udaropastha-vegam
etān vegān yo viṣaheta dhīraḥ
sarvām apīmāṁ pṛthivīṁ sa śiṣyāt

(*Upadeśāmṛta*, Verse 1)

[A wise and self-composed person who can subdue the impetus to speak, the agitation of the mind, the onset of anger, the vehemence of the tongue, the urge of the belly and the agitation of the genitals can instruct the entire world. In other words, all persons may become disciples of such a self-controlled person.]

Endnotes

1 An excerpt from *Śrī Bhakti-rasāmṛta-sindhu-bindu*, Verse 14, *Śrī Bindu-vikāśinī-vṛtti*:

When *kṛṣṇa-rati*, or in other words the *sthāyibhāva* (the permanent emotion of the heart in one of the five primary relationships of *śānta*, *dāsya*, *sakhya*, and so on), becomes exceedingly tasty for the devotee by virtue of the elements known as *vibhāva*, *anubhāva*, *sāttvika-bhāva*, and *vyābhicārī-bhāva*, induced through the medium of *śravaṇa* (hearing), *kīrtana* (chanting), and so on, it is called *bhakti-rasa*. In other words, when the *sthāyibhāva* or *kṛṣṇa-rati* mixes with *vibhāva*, *anubhāva*, *sāttvika-bhāva*, and *vyabhicāri-bhāva* and becomes fit to be tasted in the heart of the devotee, it is called *bhakti-rasa*.

Components of bhakti-rasa

Sthāyibhāva – The permanent sentiment in one of the five primary relationships of *śānta* (passive adoration), *dāsya* (servitude), *sakhya* (friendship), *vātsalya* (parental affection), or *mādhurya* (amorous), which is known as *mukhya-rati*. This also refers to the dominant sentiment in the seven secondary mellows (*gauṇa-rati*) of laughter, wonder, chivalry, compassion, anger, fear, and disgust.

Anubhāva – Visible actions that illustrate the spiritual emotions situated within the heart (dancing, singing, and so on).

Sāttvika-bhāva – Eight symptoms of spiritual ecstasy arising exclusively from *viśuddha-sattva*, or in other words, when the heart is overwhelmed by emotions in connection with *mukhya-rati* or *gauṇa-rati*.

Vyabhicāri-bhāva – Thirty-three internal spiritual emotions, which emerge from the nectarean ocean of the *sthāyibhāva*, cause it to swell, and then merge back into that ocean.

Vibhāva – That in which *rati* is tasted and the cause by which *rati* is tasted are called *vibhāva*. *Vibhāva* is of two varieties: (1) *ālambana* (the support or repository of *rati*) and (2) *uddīpana* (that which stimulates or excites *rati*).

An excerpt from Śrīla Bhaktivedānta Svāmī Mahārāja's purport to *Śrī Caitanya-caritāmṛta, Madhya-līlā* 23.51:

In *Bhakti-rasāmṛta-sindhu* (2.1.14), *vibhāva* is described as follows:

tatra jñeyā vibhāvās tu raty-āsvādana-hetavaḥ
te dvidhālambanā eke tathaivoddīpanāḥ pare

The cause bringing about the tasting of love for Kṛṣṇa is called *vibhāva*. *Vibhāva* is divided into two categories: *ālambana* (support) and *uddīpana* (awakening).

In the *Agni Purāṇa* it is stated:

vibhāvyate hi raty-ādir yatra yena vibhāvyate
vibhāvo nāma sa dvedhālambanoddīpanātmakaḥ

> That which causes love for Kṛṣṇa to appear is called *vibhāva*. That has two divisions – *ālambana* (in which love appears) and *uddīpana* (by which love appears).

In *Bhakti-rasāmṛta-sindhu* (2.1.16), the following is stated about *ālambana*:

> *kṛṣṇaś ca kṛṣṇa-bhaktāś ca budhair ālambanā matāḥ*
> *raty-āder viṣayatvena tathādhāratayāpi ca*
>
> The object of love is Kṛṣṇa, and the container of that love is the devotee of Kṛṣṇa. Learned scholars call them *ālambana* – the foundations.

Similarly, *uddīpana* is described as follows:

> *uddīpanās tu te proktā bhāvam uddīpayanti ye*
> *te tu śrī-kṛṣṇa-candrasya guṇāś ceṣṭāḥ prasādhanam*
>
> Those things which awaken ecstatic love are called *uddīpana*. Mainly this awakening is made possible by the qualities and activities of Kṛṣṇa, as well as by His mode of decoration and the way His hair is arranged (*Bhakti-rasāmṛta-sindhu* 2.1.301).

Bhakti-rasāmṛta-sindhu (2.1.302) also gives the following further examples of *uddīpana*:

> *smitāṅga-saurabhe vaṁśa-śṛṅga-nūpura-kambavaḥ*
> *padāṅka-kṣetra-tulasī-bhakta-tad-vāsarādayaḥ*
>
> Kṛṣṇa's smile, the fragrance of His transcendental body, His flute, bugle, ankle bells and conch-shell, the marks on His feet, His place of residence, His favorite plant [*tulasī*], His devotees, and the observance of fasts and vows connected to His devotion all awaken the symptoms of ecstatic love.

2 An excerpt from *Bhakti-rasāmṛta-sindhu-bindu*, Verse 7:

The ten kinds of *nāma-aparādha* will now be described in connection with the chanting of the holy name of the Lord:

(1) To commit offenses against the Vaiṣṇavas by slandering them and so on (*nindādi*). The word *ādi* here refers to the six kinds of *vaiṣṇava-aparādha* (offenses against the Vaiṣṇavas) indicated in the following verse from the *Skanda Purāṇa*, quoted in *Bhakti-sandarbha* (*Anuccheda* 265):

hanti nindati vai dveṣṭi
vaiṣṇavān nābhinandati
krudhyate yāti no harṣaṁ
darśane patanāni ṣaṭ

To beat Vaiṣṇavas, to slander them, to bear malice against them, to fail to welcome them, to become angry with them and to not feel happiness upon seeing them – by these six types of *vaiṣṇava-aparādha* one falls down to a degraded position.

(2) To consider Lord Śiva to be the Supreme Lord, separate and independent from Lord Viṣṇu.
(3) To consider *śrī gurudeva* to be an ordinary human being.
(4) To slander the Vedas, Purāṇas, and other scriptures.
(5) To consider the praises of *śrī harināma* (the holy name) to be imaginary. In other words, to consider that the potencies which have been praised in the scriptures in reference to *harināma* are not actually present in the holy name.
(6) To give an unauthorized and misleading explanation of *śrī harināma*. In other words, to abandon the established and reputed meaning of the scriptures and foolishly concoct some futile explanation. For example, someone may argue that the Lord is incorporeal (*nirākāra*), formless

(*arūpa*), and nameless (*anāma*), and that therefore His name is also imaginary.

(7) To engage in sinful activities again and again, knowing that there is such power in the holy name that simply by uttering *śrī harināma* all sins are vanquished.

(8) To consider all kinds of religious or pious activities to be equal to *śrī harināma*.

(9) To instruct faithless persons about *śrī harināma*.

(10) To not have love for the name in spite of hearing the glories of *śrī nāma*.

These ten offenses must certainly be avoided. In the practice of *hari-bhajana* (hearing, chanting, and meditating upon Śrī Kṛṣṇa's name, form, qualities, and pastimes), one should first of all be very attentive to avoid all *sevā-aparādhas* (offenses in devotional service) and *nāma-aparādhas*. One should know these offenses to be severe obstacles on the path of *bhajana* and vigorously endeavor to give them up. Without giving up these offenses there can be no question of advancement in *bhajana*; rather, the *sādhaka's* fall-down is assured.

3 An excerpt from *Ācārya Kesarī Śrī Śrīmad Bhakti Prajñāna Keśava Gosvāmī – His Life and Teachings*, Part Five:

Kṛṣṇa's *svarūpa*, or form, is composed of eternity (*sat*), knowledge (*cit*), and bliss (*ānanda*). Therefore His *svarūpa-śakti* manifests in three forms. From *ānanda* comes *hlādinī-śakti* (the pleasure potency), from *sat* comes *sandhinī* (the existence potency), and from *cit* comes *saṁvit-śakti* (the knowledge potency). *Saṁvit-śakti* is also called *jñāna-śakti*. *Hlādinī-śakti* makes Kṛṣṇa joyful (*āhlādit*), which is why its name is *hlādinī*. By this *śakti*, Kṛṣṇa, the embodiment of bliss, tastes pleasure and enables the devotees to also taste transcendental happiness. The essence of this *hlādinī* is *prema* (transcendental love), a phenomenon entirely composed of transcendental *rasa*, and is the embodiment of bliss itself. The concentrated essence of *prema* is called *mahābhāva*.[10] The embodiment of this *mahābhāva* is Śrīmatī Rādhikā. This is a summary introduction to the identity of *śakti*. [...]

What is this *bhakti*? We shall describe its intrinsic characteristic (*svarūpa-lakṣaṇa*) and its marginal characteristics (*taṭasthā-lakṣaṇa*). Its intrinsic characteristic is the full endeavor by body, mind and speech, and the cultivation of loving sentiments (*bhāva*) for the pleasure of Kṛṣṇa. Endeavors and *bhāvas* – these two remain ever-active to bring Kṛṣṇa delight. The *svarūpa-lakṣaṇa*, the intrinsic nature of *bhakti*, arises when the special function of Bhagavān's *svarūpa-śakti* (the function of the essence of *hlādinī* and *saṁvit*) appears in the *svarūpa* of the *jīva* by the mercy of Śrī Kṛṣṇa or His devotee.

4 An excerpt from *Ācārya Kesarī Śrī Śrīmad Bhakti Prajñāna Keśava Gosvāmī – His Life and Teachings*, Part Six:

The *jīva* (living entity) is spiritual, and its only natural *dharma* is spiritual service to Kṛṣṇa. The word *sahaja* means *saha-ja*, i.e., that which arises along with the *ātmā*. For the pure *ātmā*, transcendental service to Kṛṣṇa is *sahaja*, or natural, because it is intrinsic to the *jīvātmā's* constitution. However, it is not natural for one in the state of being bound by inert matter. *Sahajiyās* cheat others and are themselves cheated or deprived

---

10 "The essence of the *hlādinī-śakti* is love of Godhead, the essence of love of Godhead is *bhāva*, or transcendental sentiment, and the highest pitch of that *bhāva* is called *mahābhāva*. Śrīmatī Rādhārāṇī is the personified embodiment of these three aspects of transcendental consciousness. She is therefore the highest principle in love of Godhead and is the supreme lovable object of Śrī Kṛṣṇa"* (*Śrī Caitanya-caritāmṛta, Ādi-līlā* 4.69).

of their pure and natural love for Kṛṣṇa by saying that the mundane union of man and woman is a natural and spiritual *dharma*.

Part II

The Bona Fide Process: Śrī Śikṣāṣṭaka

The Contribution of Śrīla Bhaktivinoda Ṭhākura

The glories of Śrīla Bhaktivinoda Ṭhākura are so magnificent that even the creator of the universe, Lord Brahmā, with his four mouths, cannot completely describe them. Śrīla Bhaktivinoda Ṭhākura was a transcendental personality and we are not transcendental, so how can we touch his glories? Only a transcendental person can expound upon them.

We have heard from our *gurudeva* and other Vaiṣṇavas, and we have also read in authentic books, that Śrīla Bhaktivinoda Ṭhākura was given the title 'Seventh Gosvāmī.' From the time of the six Gosvāmīs up to his time, no one else was ever designated as such, but during his manifest stay in this world (1838–1914), learned persons and devotees saw his glorious activities and gave him this title. It was he who once again illuminated the true principles of Gauḍīya Vaiṣṇavism. If he had not appeared when he did, these pure teachings would have been forever drowned in an ocean of oblivion.

That time was a dark period for Gauḍīya Vaiṣṇavism. The *sahajiyās* used to give what they called *siddha-praṇālī*, the process, or system, that gives spiritual perfection, and even *siddha-deha* itself, to anyone and everyone, without even knowing whether or not their followers were actually devotees.

The followers neither knew any Gauḍīya Vaiṣṇava philosophy nor did they have any proper etiquette and behavior, yet they would take shelter of their *sahajiyā-bābājī gurus*, who pretended to give them their spiritual forms made of eternity, unfathomed bliss, and unlimited knowledge.

They misunderstood Śrī Caitanya Mahāprabhu's teachings. According to their conception of *siddha-deha*, Gauḍīya *bhajana* meant traveling to Vṛndāvana, living there, and having children with others' wives. They considered that by doing this they had become *gopīs*. "Come on, come on," their *guru* would say to them. "I'm giving you *siddha-deha* and *siddha-praṇālī*."

To whom did he pretend to give *siddha-deha*? Thinking, "I am this body," his disciples were totally devoid of knowledge about Śrī Caitanya Mahāprabhu's teachings. Such persons did not know that they are eternally part and parcel and servants of Kṛṣṇa. In reality, instead of being given *gopī-bhāva* they were given 'goopi' *bhāva*.

What are goopis? Goopis are lovers of this world. They think that they should find a lady, live with her, and enjoy sex life. They think this bogus *prema* to be Śrī Caitanya Mahāprabhu's philosophy.[1]

---

1 "*Prākṛta-sahajiyās* are those who understand the transcendental pastimes (*aprākṛta-līlā*) of the transcendental Supreme Lord to be *prākṛta*, or mundane, like the affairs of ordinary men and women, and who think that the *aprākṛta-tattva* (transcendental truth) is attained by a material practice" (*Ācārya Kesarī Śrī Śrīmad Bhakti Prajñāna Keśava Gosvāmī – His Life and Teachings*, Part Six).

In the name of Gauḍīya Vaiṣṇavism, these *sahajiyās* would perform Hare Kṛṣṇa *kīrtana*, following the dead body during funeral processions, and then take a large payment from the deceased's rich relatives. In their so-called *kīrtanas* the word 'Kṛṣṇa' did not clearly manifest; it was difficult for the audience to actually find the word "Kṛṣṇa." The chanters sang, "Hare Kṛṣṇa-a-a-a-a-a-a," in a fancy melody. Then the audience applauded, calling out, "Oh, very good, very good," and paid them some rupees. Although those chanters drank wine and ate meat and fish, they still imagined themselves in the realm of proper behavior, and they were still called Vaiṣṇavas by unintelligent people. Because of such disgraceful displays, learned and educated persons became ashamed and did not want to associate themselves with the words 'Gauḍīya Vaiṣṇava.'[2]

Śrīla Bhaktivinoda Ṭhākura was, in his time, the first person to preach the factual philosophy of Śrī Caitanya Mahāprabhu to this learned society. By his preaching, people came to know about true transcendental love, *prema-bhakti*.

Just as King Bhagīratha brought the Ganges River to the Earth, to India, Śrīla Bhaktivinoda Ṭhākura brought the *bhakti-gaṅga* (the flowing Ganges River of *bhakti*) to this world. Because of him, numerous people became inspired to follow pure Gauḍīya Vaiṣṇavism. If he had not appeared, we would not have joined this mission. If Śrīla Bhaktivedānta Svāmī Mahārāja had not come to the West – if he had not gone to Śrīla Bhaktisiddhānta Sarasvatī Ṭhākura and if Śrīla Bhaktisiddhānta Sarasvatī Ṭhākura had not come from Śrīla Bhaktivinoda Ṭhākura, what would have been your fate? Your good fortune is coming from Śrīla Bhaktivinoda Ṭhākura, who preached the very pure doctrines of Śrī Caitanya Mahāprabhu.

---

2 See Endnote 1, at the end of this chapter.

To Help Them

It is due to lack of intelligence, to ignorance, that these so-called *bābājīs* speak the way they do. In order to help them, Śrīla Bhaktivinoda Ṭhākura clearly explained the entire process for achieving spiritual perfection in his final literary work, *Jaiva-dharma*. In that book he clearly elucidated the qualifications for receiving full spiritual enlightenment, explaining under what circumstances the bona fide *guru* reveals *siddha-deha* to a qualified disciple; and in his book *Bhajana-rahasya*, he clarified many deep *siddhāntas* on the same subject. Those who desire entrance into the realm of *bhakti* may try to understand and follow the instructions given in *Bhajana-rahasya*, *Jaiva-dharma*, and all his other books.

As mentioned earlier, Śrīla Bhaktivinoda Ṭhākura wrote that our *bhakti* begins by our trying to serve and realize the first verse of *Śrī Śikṣāṣṭaka*: *ceto-darpaṇa-mārjanam bhava-mahā-dāvāgni-nirvāpaṇaṁ*. We then understand and practice the second verse: *nāmnām akāri bahudhā nija-sarva-śaktis*. And then the third: *tṛṇād api sunīcena taror iva sahiṣṇunā*. If we factually adopt the qualities delineated therein, we may enter the fourth: *na dhanaṁ na janaṁ na sundarīṁ*. At that time we are detached from worldly desires and tastes. When we become still more pure, when we are always chanting and remembering Kṛṣṇa without being disturbed by any obstacle, we can then enter the fifth: *ayi nanda-tanuja kiṅkaraṁ*.

Entrance into this fifth verse is the beginning of *siddha-deha*, at which time we realize ourselves as eternal servants of Kṛṣṇa in a specific relationship. The potency of a fully-grown tree is present in the seed of that tree. With water, air, and light, the seed sprouts, and gradually leaves, branches, flowers, *mañjarīs*, and finally fruits, also manifest. The entire tree or creeper is there in its seed, but all its features sprout only when air, water, and sunlight touch it. Similarly, the full potency of our eternal sentiments of love for the very Soul of all, Śrī Kṛṣṇa, is dormant in our souls, but it awakens only by adopting the pure *bhakti* process. In this fifth verse, the intrinsic form and nature of the soul is revealed.

The sixth verse of *Śrī Śikṣāṣṭaka* states:

nayanaṁ galad-aśru-dhārayā
vadanaṁ gadgada-ruddhayā girā
pulakair nicitaṁ vapuḥ kadā
tava nāma-grahaṇe bhaviṣyati

[O Prabhu! When will My eyes be filled with a stream of tears? When will My voice choke up? And when will the hairs of My body stand erect in ecstasy as I chant Your holy name?]

When a devotee realizes his *ātmā*, his pure soul, and understands that he is an eternal servant of Kṛṣṇa, he no longer has any worldly attachments. At this stage the *svarūpa-śakti*, as *hlādinī* and *saṁvit*, mercifully manifests in his heart.[3] He begins to weep, and, while chanting the holy name of Kṛṣṇa, he rolls on the earth and sings, "Agha-damana (O Kṛṣṇa, killer of the Agha demon), Yaśodānandana (O son of Yaśodā), Nanda-sūnoḥ (O, son of Nanda Mahārāja), where are You?"

The devotee may sometimes get a glimpse of Kṛṣṇa and immediately run towards Him. And then, when Kṛṣṇa goes out of sight, that devotee rolls on the ground in separation. Without our feeling this type of separation, our constitutional form does not manifest. Those who artificially exhibit emotions of separation will go to hell, like the thousands of *sahajiyā bābājīs* in Vṛndāvana and Rādhā-kuṇḍa who are simply illicitly giving birth to children and engaging in other malpractices.

---

3 Please see Endnote 3, at the end of Part 1 (p 24).

One of the brothers of Śrīla Bhaktisiddhānta Sarasvatī Ṭhākura used to think that his father, Śrīla Bhaktivinoda Ṭhākura, was his physical body. In fact, he thought of himself as the son of Kedarnātha Daṭṭa (Śrīla Bhaktivinoda Ṭhākura's civil name), not Śrīla Bhaktivinoda Ṭhākura. On the other hand, Śrīla Bhaktisiddhānta Sarasvatī Ṭhākura considered his father to be an associate of Śrī Kṛṣṇa, Śrīmatī Rādhārāṇī, and Śrī Caitanya Mahāprabhu. He never considered him his material father, a person made of blood and flesh. Śrīla Bhaktisiddhānta Sarasvatī Ṭhākura actually followed the path of Śrīla Bhaktivinoda Ṭhākura. Whatever his father spoke, he fully accepted and followed.

Our goal is *siddha-deha*, but what is *siddha-deha*? And what is *siddha-praṇālī* (the process that bestows spiritual perfection)? Who started the *bābājī* version of *siddha-deha*, in what year did it begin, and from where did it originate? Śrīla Sanātana Gosvāmī and Śrīla Rūpa Gosvāmī are called Gosvāmī, not Bābājī. No one has given them the title Rūpa Bābājī, Sanātana Bābājī, or Śrīla Raghunātha dāsa Bābājī. At the time of Śrīla Viśvanātha Cakravartī Ṭhākura, no one addressed him as Viśvanātha Cakravartī Bābājī. During his time, the process of giving someone this bogus version of *gopī-bhāva* was not practiced. No one gave this *bābājī siddha-praṇālī* to them.

What is *siddha-praṇālī*? *Siddha-praṇālī* is *Śikṣāṣṭaka* – from the first verse. In order to follow the third verse, beginning *tṛṇād api sunīcena*, one requires this awareness: "I am the eternal servant of Śrī Kṛṣṇa, Śrī Caitanya Mahāprabhu, and Śrī Nityānanda Prabhu." Upon this platform of understanding, that devotee becomes detached from worldly attractions and chants and remembers Kṛṣṇa twenty-four hours a day under the guidance of any very qualified Vaiṣṇava.

tan-nāma-rūpa-caritādi-sukīrtanānu-
smṛtyoḥ krameṇa rasanā-manasī niyojya

tiṣṭhan vraje tad-anurāgi-janānugāmī
kālaṁ nayed akhilam ity upadeśa-sāram
(*Upadeśāmṛta*, Verse 8)

[While living in Vraja as a follower of the eternal residents of Vraja, who possess inherent spontaneous love for Śrī Kṛṣṇa, one should utilize all his time by sequentially engaging the tongue and the mind in meticulous chanting and remembrance of Kṛṣṇa's names, form, qualities, and pastimes. This is the essence of all instruction.]

Śrīla Raghunātha dāsa Gosvāmī has explained this *siddha-praṇālī* in his prayer called *Manaḥ-śikṣā*. All the verses of his prayer are *praṇālī*, not artificial imaginings.

From where and from whom has this artificial *siddha-deha* come? There is no history. It is not in our culture, nor is it the teaching of Śrī Caitanya Mahāprabhu. Real *siddha-deha* and *siddha-praṇālī* manifest when we follow the correct process – beginning with taking complete shelter of *guru* (*guru-kāraṇa*), worshiping him (*guru-bhajana*), serving him under his direction (*guru-sevā*), and after that, *bhajana-praṇālī*. It comes by adopting, with purity, the process of hearing, chanting, remembering the Lord, serving the Lord's lotus feet, worshiping Him, offering Him prayers, becoming His servant, becoming His friend, and surrendering everything to Him. It comes by:

sādhu-saṅga, nāma-kīrtana, bhāgavata-śravaṇa
mathurā-vāsa, śrī-mūrtira śraddhāya sevana
(*Śrī Caitanya-caritāmṛta, Madhya-līlā* 22.128)

[In the association of devotees one should chant the holy name of the Lord, hear *Śrīmad-Bhāgavatam*, reside in Mathurā, and worship the Deity with faith and reverence.]

By our following these processes, Śrī Kṛṣṇa and Śrīmatī Rādhikā will mercifully give us our perfect form, that form which is fit to serve Them.

How Śrī Nārada Muni Received Siddha-deha

Śrīmad-Bhāgavatam states that Nārada Muni received his *mantra* from Sanaka, Sanandana, Sanātana, and Sanat-kumāra. Later, as soon as his mother died, he left for the dense forest. There he bathed in a river, sat down silently under the shade of a *banyan* tree, chanted his *mantra*, and meditated upon the Supersoul within his heart. After practicing this for many years, Lord Viṣṇu momentarily manifested in his heart and then vanished.

As mentioned earlier, Nārada wept bitterly in separation from Lord Viṣṇu, and then a voice from the sky called to him, "Nārada, I will not give you *darśana* again as long as you are in this material body. Continue chanting My name, remembering Me, and glorifying My pastimes all over the world. At the appropriate time, when death comes, you will put your feet on the head of death and be liberated." [4]

Following Viṣṇu's instruction, Nārada always chanted and remembered the Lord, and while playing on his *vīṇā*, he sang songs and poems glorifying the pastimes of Kṛṣṇa. For example, he sang *rādhā-ramaṇa haribol*. Śrīla Bhaktivinoda Ṭhākura also wrote about many pastimes of Kṛṣṇa and His devotees in his own poetries and songs. He wrote a song beginning, "*nārada-muni, bājāya vīṇā, rādhikā-ramaṇa-nāme* – Nārada Muni plays his *vīṇā* while chanting the glories of Rādhā and Kṛṣṇa."

---

4 This means that when Nārada will leave his body at the time of death, he will not suffer any pain or unhappiness, as do ordinary conditioned souls. Moreover, he will immediately attain his eternal spiritual form and eternal service to the Lord –Ed.

He also wrote:

yaśomatī-nandana, braja-baro-nāgara,
gokula-rañjana kāna
gopī-parāṇa-dhana, madana-manohara,
kālīya-damana-vidhāna

[Kṛṣṇa is the beloved son of Mother Yaśodā, the topmost hero of Vraja, the delight of Gokula, and Kāna (an affectionate nickname for Kṛṣṇa). He is the treasure of the lives of the *gopīs*, the enchanter of even Cupid, and the punisher of the serpent Kāliya.]

After many years, Nārada left his mortal body. At that same moment his *siddha-deha* manifested, and in that *siddha-deha* he became so powerful that he could travel anywhere in the universe or beyond. Unlike Dhruva Mahārāja, Nārada did not require the help of an airplane to transport him to Vaikuṇṭha.

We should try to know all of the processes taught by Śrīla Bhaktivinoda Ṭhākura.[5] This particular process is given when the disciple is in an advanced stage of *bhakti*: *śravaṇa-daśā* (the stage of hearing), *varaṇa-daśā* (the stage of thirsting for spiritual emotions), *smaraṇa-daśā* (the stage of remembrance of the Lord and His intimate associates)[6], *bhāvāpaña-daśā* (the stage of uninterrupted remembrance and ecstatic spiritual sentiments in *bhāva-bhakti*, or *svarūpa-siddhi*), and finally *prema-sampatti-daśā* (attaining the ultimate goal, love of Godhead). It is in *sampatti-daśā* that one fully realizes his *siddha-deha* (this stage is also known as *vastu-siddhi*, the spiritual body receiving direct *darśana* and service of the Lord and His associates)[7].

---

5 This is given especially in Śrīla Bhaktivinoda Ṭhākura's *Śrī Harināma-cintāmaṇi* and *Jaiva-dharma*.

6 See Endnote 2, at the end of this chapter.

7 See Endnote 3, at the end of this chapter.

In *śravaṇa-daśā*, the stage of hearing, one hears about the process to attain perfection from his bona fide *guru* from Vedic scriptures like *Śrīmad-Bhāgavatam, Śrī Caitanya-caritāmṛta, Jaiva-dharma*, and the entire philosophy of Śrīla Rūpa Gosvāmī. In *śravaṇa-daśā* there are many things to learn, such as one's name and identity – not the name of one's material body, but of his transcendental body.

The true *guru* knows this. A false *guru* does not know this, but by imagination gives this type of information. The bona fide *guru* knows everything: your name, your relationship with Śrī Kṛṣṇa, Śrīmatī Rādhikā, and the *gopīs*, your place of residence – whether it is at Rādhā-kuṇḍa, Jāvaṭa, Nandagaon, or Varṣāṇa – the name of your father and mother, your service, and the nature of your beautiful form. He then reveals your particular service to Rādhā-Kṛṣṇa conjugal, and your *pālya-dāsī-bhāva*, your nature as a maidservant of Śrīmatī Rādhikā. As mentioned earlier, there are eleven items in all.

Taste in the Name and Mercy to All

To teach this actual process was the main objective of Śrīla Bhaktivinoda Ṭhākura, whose teachings he personally summarized in two lines: "*jīva dayā kṛṣṇa-nāma, sarva-dharma-sāra* – Shower mercy on all the *jīvas*, seeing them as Śrī Kṛṣṇa's, and completely surrender unto the Holy Name of Śrī Kṛṣṇa. This is the essence of all religious principles." This is also the sum and substance of all the teachings of all the Vedas, Vedānta, Upaniṣads, *Bhagavad-gītā*, the Purāṇas, Śrutis, Smṛtis, and Pañcarātra.

In essence, there are two principles: *jīva dayā* and *kṛṣṇa-nāma*. The meaning of *jīva dayā* is 'mercy to conditioned souls.' Śrīla Bhaktivinoda Ṭhākura has elaborately explained that the best *dayā*, or mercy, is turning conditioned souls from their worldly moods to the mood of service to Kṛṣṇa. It is worth more than opening hundreds of thousands of hospitals and universities, or donating hundreds of thousands of dollars in charity. *Jīva-dayā* is the most special gift, and it is given by the realized soul.

harer nāma harer nāma harer nāmaiva kevalam
kalau nāsty eva nāsty eva nāsty eva gatir anyathā
(*Śrī Caitanya-caritāmṛta, Ādi-līlā* 17.21)

[In this age of quarrel and hypocrisy, the only means of deliverance is the chanting of the holy name of the Lord. There is no other way. There is no other way. There is no other way.*]

Jīva dayā is attained only by chanting Kṛṣṇa's holy name. Kṛṣṇa's name is Kṛṣṇa Himself, but we can chant *śuddha-nāma*, the pure name devoid of all offenses and misconceptions on the part of the chanter, only in the association of the bona fide *guru* and bona fide Vaiṣṇavas. Without this association we can neither chant the pure name nor engage in pure *śuddha-bhakti*.

What is *śuddha-bhakti*, or pure devotion? We may think that *vaidhī-bhakti*, devotion prompted by the regulations of the scriptures, is *śuddha-bhakti*, but it is not, nor will it ever become so. *Śuddha-bhakti* is *rāgānuga-bhakti*, or devotion impelled by greed to follow in the footsteps of the personal associates of Śrī Śrī Rādhā-Kṛṣṇa.[8] When the practice of *rāgānuga-bhakti* fully matures, it is then called *rāgātmika-prema*, or the love of Kṛṣṇa's associates in Vṛndāvana. In other words, when the sincere devotee desires *rāgātmika-prema*, he cultivates its attainment with all of his senses; this is called *rāgānuga*, or devotion performed in the wake of the *rāgātmika-bhaktas*.

---

8 See Endnote 4, at the end of this chapter.

When one's heart accepts the same mood that Śrīla Rūpa Gosvāmī possesses, the mood of a *pālya-dāsī* of Śrīmatī Rādhikā, this is called *rūpānuga-bhakti*.

We conditioned souls are eligible to become *pālya-dāsīs*, maidservants of Śrīmatī Rādhikā. We cannot become like Lalitā or Viśākhā, whose position as direct beloveds of Kṛṣṇa is beyond our limit of attainment. We can follow only Śrīla Rūpa Gosvāmī or Rūpa Mañjarī, Rati Mañjarī, Lavaṅga Mañjarī, and all the other *mañjarīs*. The *sahajiyā bābājīs'* utterance of "Oh, you are Lalitā. I am Lalitā," is nothing but *māyāvāda* philosophy (the doctrine of illusion and impersonalism) or monism – artificial imitation.

Śrīla Bhaktivinoda Ṭhākura foretold that in the near future many hundreds of thousands of Western devotees with *śikhā* and *tulasī-mālā* will meet with Indian devotees, and they will all chant together, "*haribol, haribol*," "*gaura premānande hari haribol*," and, "*hare kṛṣṇa hare kṛṣṇa kṛṣṇa kṛṣṇa hare hare / hare rāma hare rāma rāma rāma hare hare*." Thus, all over the world the pure mission of Śrī Caitanya Mahāprabhu will spread. This idea was started by Śrīla Bhaktivinoda Ṭhākura. He is the root of all our preaching, and therefore we are truly indebted to him.

Endnotes

1 An excerpt from *Ācārya Kesarī Śrī Śrīmad Bhakti Prajñāna Keśava Gosvāmī – His Life and Teachings*, Part Six:

After Śrīla Viśvanātha Cakravartī Ṭhākura and Baladeva Vidyābhūṣaṇa, a dark age began in Śrīman Mahāprabhu's Gauḍīya *sampradāya*, during which the current of *śrī rūpānuga-bhakti* became somewhat impaired. Various kinds of speculative malpractices and opinions opposed to *śuddha-bhakti* seeped into the true conception. At that time the situation became so dire that the educated and cultured section of society began to abhor even the name of Gauḍīya Vaiṣṇavism, having witnessed the misconduct of its so-called followers. In this way the Gauḍīya Vaiṣṇava *sampradāya* became distanced from the intelligentsia and respected society.

2 An excerpt from *Śrī Bhajana-rahasya*, Chapter 6, Text 7:

Because meditative remembrance (*smaraṇa*) is predominant in spontaneous devotion (*rāgānuga-bhakti*), some persons, who still have *anarthas* and in whose hearts genuine attachment to Kṛṣṇa has not yet appeared, make a deceitful display of solitary *bhajana* and, considering themselves *rāgānuga* devotees, they practice what they call *aṣṭa-kālīya-līlā-smaraṇa*. However, *Bhakti-rasāmṛta-sindhu* (1.2.101) quotes from the *āgama-śāstras* as follows:

śruti-smṛti-purāṇādi-
pañcarātra-vidhiṁ vinā
aikāntikī harer bhaktir
utpātāyaiva kalpate

> If a person violates the regulations mentioned in the Śruti, Smṛti, Purāṇas, and the *Nārada-pañcarātra*, great misgivings (*anarthas*) are produced, even though he may be engaged in one-pointed devotion to Hari.

3 An excerpt from *Śrī Harināma-cintāmaṇi*, Chapter 15:

When a *sādhaka* devotee, having heard about Lord Kṛṣṇa's pastimes, is attracted to the conjugal mellow, he should take further instruction on *rasa* from a realized, saintly spiritual master. This is called the stage of hearing or *śravaṇa-daśā*. When the *sādhaka* devotee anxiously and eagerly accepts the conjugal mellow, *varaṇa-daśā* commences. Then, by pure remembrance of the sentiments of *rasa*, he desires to practice them; he then reaches the third stage, *smaraṇa-daśā*. When he is able to perfectly invoke these sentiments of *rasa*, he attains *āpana-daśā*, or *prāpti-daśā*. Finally, when he can separate himself from all his temporal material designations and is steadily fixed in that original spiritual identity for which he yearns, he has reached *sampatti-daśā* – the inheritance of his spiritual identity.

4 An excerpt from a lecture by Śrīla Bhaktivedānta Svāmī Mahārāja on *Śrīmad-Bhāgavatam* 1.2.33, spoken in Vṛndāvana on November 12, 1972:

So you have to uncover. You have to discover. That discovering process is devotional service. The more you are engaged in devotional service, the more your senses become pure or uncovered. And when they are completely uncovered, without any designation, then you are capable to serve Kṛṣṇa. This is apprenticeship. *Vaidhī-bhakti* (devotion prompted by the regulations of the scriptures).

***Śrī Caitanya-caritāmṛta, Madhya-līlā* 22.149 states:**

The original inhabitants of Vṛndāvana are attached to Kṛṣṇa spontaneously in devotional service. Nothing can compare to such spontaneous devotional service, which is called *rāgātmika-bhakti*. When a devotee follows in the footsteps of the devotees of Vṛndāvana, his devotional service is called *rāgānuga-bhakti*.

Part III

The Sahajiyā Bābājīs

No Guru-paramparā, No Śāstric Reference

I offer my many hundreds of thousands of *daṇḍavat praṇāmas*, my humble obeisance, unto the lotus feet of my *gurudeva, nitya-līlā-praviṣṭa oṁ viṣṇupāda* Śrī Śrīmad Bhakti Prajñāna Keśava Gosvāmī Mahārāja. I also offer my hundreds of thousands of *daṇḍavat praṇāmas* unto the lotus feet of my *śikṣā-guru*, Śrī Śrīmad Bhaktivedānta Svāmī Mahārāja, who preached the mission of pure *bhakti* throughout the world in a very short time. By his mercy we are able to know Śrī Śrī Rādhā and Kṛṣṇa, and Śrī Caitanya Mahāprabhu and His teachings.

Some *bābājīs* in Vraja-Vṛndāvana are saying that Śrīla Bhaktivedānta Svāmī Mahārāja and other bona fide disciples of Śrīla Bhaktisiddhānta Sarasvatī Gosvāmī Ṭhākura do not have a *guru-paramparā*, a disciplic succession of bona fide *gurus*. These foolish and weak persons, knowing nothing of *śāstra* (Vedic scripture), are bewildered in this way.

[Our entire *paramparā* descended to this world from Goloka Vṛndāvana, and Śrīla Bhaktisiddānta Sarasvatī Ṭhākura was one of the most prominent *ācāryas*. If he had not come, everything would have been transferred into *sahajiyāism* – wherein all philosophy is *asat-sampradāya*, outside the *paramparā* line of philosophy, spiritual sentiments and behavior.

If one is not serving his *gurudeva*, if he does not have strong belief in his *gurudeva*, and if he is not following his *gurudeva's* line of thought, such a person must be *sahajiyā*. This is taking place nowadays. We are preaching and therefore the *sahajiyās* are somewhat stopped, but I do not know what will happen after I leave this world. A very dangerous stage is coming.

Many ISKCON devotees left Śrīla Bhaktivedānta Svāmī Mahārāja, their *gurudeva*, Śrīla Prabhupāda, and they went to Rādhā-kuṇḍa. They wanted to remember the twenty-four-hour daily amorous pastimes of Śrī Śrī Rādhā and Kṛṣṇa (*aṣṭa-kālīya-līlā*) as goopīs – not *gopīs*, but goopīs – and for this offense they went to hell.][1]

A personality who can preach the mission of Caitanya Mahāprabhu throughout the world in a very short time, who can translate and write commentaries to authentic books like *Śrī Caitanya-caritāmṛta*, who can publish and explain *Śrīmad-Bhāgavatam* and the books of Śrīla Rūpa Gosvāmī and Śrīla Jīva Gosvāmī – how can he be an ordinary person? He was certainly in the line of Śrīla Bhaktivinoda Ṭhākura, Śrīla Raghunātha dāsa Gosvāmī, Śrīla Rūpa Gosvāmī, Svarūpa Dāmodara, Rāya Rāmānanda, and Śrī Caitanya Mahāprabhu.

No one can say from where the *bābājīs' guru-paramparā* has come, and actually they have no *guru-paramparā*. This is why they blaspheme real Vaiṣṇavas in the *guru-paramparā*. The word '*bābājī*' is not found in any scripture.[2] Neither

1 This insertion is an excerpt from Śrīla Bhaktivedānta Nārāyaṇa Gosvāmī Mahārāja's morning lecture, spoken in Olpe, Germany, on February 21, 2003.

2 The word '*bābājī*' is a homonym, in that the current use of *bābājī*, as referred to here, has a different meaning from the true sense of the word *bābājī*. Śrīla Gurudeva, Śrī Śrīmad Bhaktivedānta Nārāyaṇa Gosvāmī Mahārāja, discusses elsewhere in this book that in classical Indian culture, the word *bābājī* was a

Vedic scriptures like *Bhagavad-gītā*, the Purāṇas, Upaniṣads, Vedānta, Baladeva Vidyābhūṣaṇa's *Govinda-bhāṣya*, nor the books of great *ācāryas* like Śrīla Viśvanātha Cakravartī Ṭhākura and Śrīla Narottama Ṭhākura mention the word *bābājī*. On the other hand, we see the words 'renounced order' and '*sannyāsa*.' *Bhagavad-gītā* explains the qualification of the true *sannyāsī*, and the Vedas and *Śrīmad-Bhāgavatam* discuss the history of *tridaṇḍi sannyāsa*. In the Upaniṣads, the method by which a person can take the renounced order, *sannyāsa*, by accepting saffron cloth, *daṇḍa* (the rod carried by *sannyāsīs*), and *ḍor-kaupīna*[3] has been clearly given; in fact, one of the Upaniṣads is called *Sannyāsa Upaniṣad*.[4]

There is no mention in any of these Vedic Scriptures about *bābājīs*. Śrī Caitanya Mahāprabhu was not a *bābājī*, nor were Madhvācārya and Rāmānuja. Īśvara Purīpāda and Mādhavendra Purī were not *bābājīs*; they were *sannyāsīs*, and after them, Sanātana Gosvāmī, Svarūpa Dāmodara, and Rāya Rāmānanda were also not *bābājīs*.

---

respectful way of addressing a saintly person. ... (Continued on the next page) ... Examples of this are Śrīla Gaura Kiśora dāsa Bābājī Mahārāja and Śrīla Jagannātha dāsa Bābājī Mahārāja. In *Jaiva-dharma* we read of the Gauḍīya Vaiṣṇava *gurus* Prema dāsa Bābājī and Raghunātha dāsa Bābājī. Śrīla Sanātana Gosvāmī was referred to by the villagers of Vṛndāvana as *bara-bābā*, or 'elder *sādhu*,' and they referred to Śrīla Rūpa Gosvāmī as *choṭa-bābā*, or 'young *sādhu*.' *Bābā* is also a term of address for 'Father,' as in the case of Śrī Kṛṣṇa's own father, Nanda Bābā.

When Śrīla Gurudeva says, "The word *bābājī* is not found in any scripture," he is referring to the kind of *bābājī* who imagines that he is a perfected devotee and can give that same 'perfection' to his unqualified disciple through a concocted process of a *mantra* and *bābājī* initiation.

Nowadays, there are also *māyāvādī gurus* who call themselves *bābā* and proclaim that they are God or that we are all God. The reader will be able to understand which type of *bābājī* Śrīla Gurudeva has indicated by the context –Ed.]

3 *Ḍor* and *kaupīna* are two cloths that signify one's renunciation from material sense gratification.

4 See Endnote 1, at the end of this chapter.

Has Śrīla Rūpa Gosvāmī taken a *bābājī* initiation from anyone? Has he taken *ḍor-kaupīna* initiation?[5] He wore an ordinary white cloth. It is not written anywhere that he did so.[6]

Jīva Gosvāmī was Jīva Gosvāmī, not Jīva Bābājī. Kṛṣṇadāsa Kavirāja Gosvāmī kept his name from his *gṛhastha āśrama*, and Śyāmānanda prabhu, Narottama Ṭhākura, and Śrīnivāsa Ācārya were also not *bābājīs*. They were not in that line of cheapening the idea of *bhakti*: "You are such-and-such goopi."[7] Similarly, until the end of his life, Śrīla Viśvanātha Cakravartī Ṭhākura was Viśvanātha Cakravartī Ṭhākura, keeping the title of *gṛhastha* (householder) Vaiṣṇava *brāhmaṇas* (the priests or teachers of divine knowledge).[8] In addition, his disciple Baladeva Vidyābhūṣaṇa was also not *bābājī*.

Actually, in its proper context, the word *bābājī* was used for old persons in villages. For example, someone would say to Sanātana Gosvāmī, "O, *bara* (elder) *bābājī*."

Mahāprabhu's Guru-paramparā

When Śrī Caitanya Mahāprabhu was in Vārāṇasī, Kāśī, Śrīla Sanātana Gosvāmī came to meet Him for the first time - with a big beard, wearing very dirty clothing, and looking like a Mohammedan beggar. Still, when Caitanya Mahāprabhu saw him, He at once ran towards him and embraced him. After that He ordered Sanātana Gosvāmī to take bath in the Ganges, and to shave. Mahāprabhu's associate Tapāna Miśra soon arrived there, desiring to give Sanātana Gosvāmī new cloth, but Sanātana Gosvāmī refused, saying, "If you want to give me clothing, please give me your old *dhotī*." From this old *dhotī* cloth,

5 Rūpa Gosvāmī adopted this dress himself –Ed.

6 See Endnote 2, at the end of this chapter.

7 Please see page 28 for an explanation of the word 'goopi.'

8 When he left home to become renounced, he was also known as Śrī Hariballabha dāsa – Ed.

Sanātana Gosvāmī made his outer cloth and the *ḍor-kaupīna* of the *sannyāsīs*. There was no fire sacrifice or Vedic ritual for this, nor did Caitanya Mahāprabhu give him any *mantra* for this.[9]

Seeing Caitanya Mahāprabhu dressed in the saffron cloth of a *sannyāsī*, Sanātana Gosvāmī considered, "I should be very humble. I should not wear the same color cloth as Caitanya Mahāprabhu." He had great honor for that *sannyāsī* cloth and *daṇḍa*, and therefore, being a humble person, he wore only a very small piece of white cloth, to minimize his bodily necessities. He did not want to wear a long *dhotī* and *kurtā* as a fashion. He wore only the minimum required.[10]

Qualifications of Guru and Disciple

It is not written anywhere that Caitanya Mahāprabhu gave 'goopi-*bhāva*,' telling anyone and everyone, "Now you are a goopi, and I am now giving you the eleven kinds of moods. Your name is Lalitā, your birthplace is Varṣāṇā, you are married to such-and-such *gopa*, your dress is such-and-such, and you are a *pālya-dāsī* from today onwards." He never did this.

Can one who is simply engaged in the animalistic propensities of eating, sleeping, mating, and defending, and in the three W's of wine, woman, and wealth – can he be given *gopī-bhāva*? This *sahajiyāism* is the root of all evil.

Gauḍīya Vaiṣṇavism begins from the origin: from Brahmā to Nārada, Vyāsa, Śukadeva Gosvāmī, Madhvācārya and his *paramparā*, or disciplic succession, and then to Mādhavendra Purī, Isvara Purī, Caitanya Mahāprabhu, Rūpa-Sanātana, Jīva, Raghunātha, Kṛṣṇadāsa Kavirāja Gosvāmī, Narottama Ṭhākura, and Śyāmānanda, and after that to Viśvanātha Cakravartī Ṭhākura. This is the line of our Gauḍīya *guru-paramparā*.

---

9 See Endnote 3, at the end of this chapter.

10 See Endnote 4, at the end of this chapter.

Some persons challenge Śrīla Bhaktivinoda Ṭhākura, demanding, "Who was his *guru*?" Actually, he accepted Vipina Bihārī Gosvāmī as his *dīkṣā-guru*, initiating spiritual master, in the line of *pāñcarātrika guru-paramparā*[11], and he has written in his *Śrī Caitanya-caritāmṛta* commentary that his *śikṣā bhāgavata-paramparā*[12] *guru*, his instructing spiritual master, was Jagannātha dāsa Bābājī Mahārāja. *Śikṣā-guru* is not less than *dīkṣā-guru*, and sometimes he may be more than *dīkṣā-guru*. For example, we accept Caitanya Mahāprabhu, Rādhā-Kṛṣṇa, and Rūpa Gosvāmī as our *śikṣā-gurus*, as Kṛṣṇadāsa Kavirāja Gosvāmī accepted the six Gosvāmīs as his *śikṣā-gurus*:

śrī-rūpa, sanātana, bhaṭṭa-raghunātha
śrī-jīva, gopāla-bhaṭṭa, dāsa-raghunātha

ei chaya guru—śikṣā-guru ye āmāra
tāṅ'-sabāra pāda-padme koṭi namaskāra

(*Śrī Caitanya-caritāmṛta, Ādi-līlā* 1.36–37)

[Śrī Rūpa Gosvāmī, Śrī Sanātana Gosvāmī, Śrī Bhaṭṭa Raghunātha, Śrī Jīva Gosvāmī, Śrī Gopāla Bhaṭṭa Gosvāmī, and Śrīla Raghunātha dāsa Gosvāmī; these six are my instructing spiritual masters, and therefore I offer millions of respectful obeisances unto their lotus feet.]

There need be no doubt in this connection, that sometimes the *śikṣā-guru* may be superior to the *dīkṣā-guru*. For example, I have so much faith in my *gurudeva*, but I know that Rūpa Gosvāmī is *guru* of my *gurudeva*. Similarly, although Śrīla Bhaktisiddhānta Sarasvatī Ṭhākura is our *jagad-guru*, he

---

11 The disciplic line based on receiving formal *mantras* –Ed.

12 The succession of bona fide *gurus* rooted in receiving and following transcendental instructions from their predecessors –Ed.

personally considered Rūpa Gosvāmī and Śrīmatī Rādhikā to be his *śikṣā-gurus*.

Śrī Bilvamaṅgala Ṭhākura has prayed in his book, *Kṛṣṇa-karṇāmṛta*:

cintāmaṇir jayati somagirir gurur me
śikṣā-guruś ca bhagavān śikhi-piñcha-mauliḥ
yat-pāda-kalpataru-pallava-śekhareṣu
līlā-svayaṁvara-rasaṁ labhate jayaśrīḥ

[All glories to Cintāmaṇi, and my initiating spiritual master, Somagiri. All glories to my instructing spiritual master, the Supreme Personality of Godhead, who wears peacock feathers in His crown. Under the shade of His lotus feet, which are like desire trees, Jayaśrī (Rādhārāṇī) enjoys the transcendental mellow of an eternal consort.]

Bilvamaṅgala Ṭhākura states here that his *śikṣā-guru* is Kṛṣṇa, Nanda-nandana Himself, with peacock feathers in His turban and a flute to His lips. Bilvamaṅgala Ṭhākura's *dīkṣā-guru* was Somagiri, but he gave more preference to his *śikṣā-guru*, Śrī Kṛṣṇa. He had faith in his *dīkṣā-guru*, but at the same time he respected his *śikṣā-guru* as superior. We should not forget these truths.

Can you say who was the *guru* of Śrīla Haridāsa Ṭhākura? When Brahmā and Prahlāda Mahārāja combine together in the form of Caitanya Mahāprabhu's associate (Śrīla Haridāsa Ṭhākura), he doesn't need any formal initiation. Can you say who was the *guru* of Svarūpa Dāmodara or Srīvāsa Paṇḍita? Śrīvāsa Paṇḍita is Nārada Ṛṣi, and Murāri Gupta is Hanumān. Perhaps they were initiated by someone else, but Caitanya Mahāprabhu accepted them all as His own. Similarly, although we may not know who their *guru* is, we also accept them as bona fide.

Similarly, we need have no doubt about Śrīla Bhaktivedānta Svāmī Mahārāja, thinking that he has no *guru-paramparā*. His *dīkṣā-guru* was Śrīla Bhaktisiddhānta Sarasvatī Ṭhākura Prabhupāda. Śrīla Bhaktisiddhānta Sarasvatī's *dīkṣā-guru* was Śrīla Gaura Kiśora dāsa Bābājī Mahārāja, and his *śikṣā-guru* was Śrīla Bhaktivinoda Ṭhākura. He accepted as his *dīkṣā-guru* Śrīla Gaura Kiśora dāsa Bābājī Mahārāja, who was not only a pure Vaiṣṇava, but a *mahā-bhāgavata*, the greatest of pure devotees, and he received so much instruction from him regarding *bhajana*. At the same time, he received most of his conceptions for *bhajana* from Śrīla Bhaktivinoda Ṭhākura, as well as all his conceptions for establishing and spreading the principles of pure *bhakti* in this world.

Pāñcarātrika Guru-paramparā and Bhāgavata-paramparā

Without *bhāgavata-paramparā*[13], *guru-paramparā*[14] is nothing.[15] Regarding Śrīla Bhaktivinoda Ṭhākura, even if he were to have had no *dīkṣā-guru*, as was the case with Śrīla Haridāsa Ṭhākura and others, still he is a pure Vaiṣṇava. But he did have a *dīkṣā-guru*.

We have no doubt that he was in *paramparā*, whereas a doubtful person loses whatever *bhakti* he has and goes to hell. The jealous *bābājīs* are like that. Although they cannot say where their own *paramparā* began, they very easily say, "Gauḍīya Vaiṣṇavas have no *paramparā*." Moreover, it is bogus persons who, shaking like a pendulum (engaged in going back and forth

---

13 The disciplic succession of *mahā-bhāgavata gurus* wherein the disciple accepts his *guru's* mood and *siddhānta* irrespective of formal initiation. –Ed.

14 The disciplic succession of *gurus* who may or may not be *mahā-bhāgavatas*, and from whom one accepts formal initiation. –Ed.

15 See Endnote 5, at the end of this chapter.

between renunciation and material enjoyment), rejected by Gauḍīya Vaiṣṇavas, being debauchees with an abundance of lust – it is they who have become these *bābājīs*.

Be very strong in the proper understanding. Śrīla Bhaktivinoda Ṭhākura, Śrīla Prabhupāda, Śrīla Bhaktivedānta Svāmī Mahārāja, and also us – we don't want to criticize these so-called *bābājīs'* avoidance of rules and regulations or their keeping *bābājī-veśa*. What we criticize is their mood. Bhaktivinoda Ṭhākura has not criticized their dress of *ḍor-kaupīna*, or even that they falsely claim, "We are following the *gopīs*."

We criticize – Śrīla Bhaktivinoda Ṭhākura, Śrīla Prabhupāda Bhaktisiddhānta Sarasvatī Ṭhākura, Śrīla Rūpa Gosvāmī, and all other bona fide *ācāryas* have criticized – that a newcomer who barely knows *śāstra* (Vedic scripture) or *siddhānta*, who is quarreling with his wife, or his wife has divorced him and he has no means to support his life, comes to these *bābājīs* and thinks, "If I take *bābājī-veśa*, everything will be solved. I may also have two, three, four, or five widows; no harm. I will then be equipped with all things necessary for worldly life."[16]

They show no symptoms of renunciation, and they are ignorant to the extreme regarding established truth. They don't know what *bhakti* is, what *bhakti-rasa* is, or even who Kṛṣṇa is and who the *gopīs* are. Full of envy, they are always engaged in association of sense gratifiers. Still, if they see someone receptive at Rādhā-kuṇḍa or Vṛndāvana, they take twenty-five *paisā* from them and think that they themselves are making a *guru-paramparā*. Such a so-called *guru* does this at once, without delay, thinking that otherwise, ignorant people will go to another *bābājī* to become his disciple. Therefore he at once makes them shave off their hair, at once gives them *ḍor* and *kaupīna*, and at once givesa so-called *gopī* mood: "You are Lalitā," or, "You are Rūpa Mañjarī," or, "You are such-and-such Mañjarī."

16 See Endnote 6, at the end of this chapter.

As mentioned earlier, the correct method is that the candidate first tries to obey all the rules and regulations of the householder *āśrama*. He then becomes detached from worldly affairs and, receiving the association of Vaiṣṇava *sādhus*, comes to *śraddhā*, more *sādhu-saṅga*, and then properly understands the need of *sad-guru*. He will then inquire and search for a qualified *guru*. He will take initiation from him, as well as teachings and instructions. He will engage in *viśrambheṇa guroḥ sevā*, serving him with intimacy and affection. He will serve *gurudeva* in a beautiful way, like a friend.

He will offer himself totally to *gurudeva*, and after many days or many years he will become qualified in all kinds of basic and elevated *bhakti-siddhānta*, conclusive truths. He will learn *Bhakti-sandarbha* and the entire *Śrīmad-Bhāgavatam*, and then he will be qualified to come to the stage of *niṣṭhā*. Then, after completing his course of *niṣṭhā*, *ruci* will come naturally and automatically. *Ruci* manifests toward *bhajana* – chanting, and remembering – and is of two kinds.[17] *Āśakti* comes then, and it is also of two kinds. First it will manifest as *āsakti* in chanting and remembering, and then it will turn into *āsakti* towards Rādhā-Kṛṣṇa and Caitanya Mahāprabhu personally.

At that time the candidate will be qualified to take *ḍor-kaupīna* and the *ekādaśa bhāvas* (eleven moods), and at that stage *śrī guru* will help him in manifesting his ecstatic spiritual form; at that very stage, not before. At that stage the bona fide *guru* tells his qualified disciple, "You are so-and-so and your *siddha* name is such-and-such." He is not doing anything externally, meaning that he is not changing the disciple's *veśa* (dress) or *āśrama* (any one of the four stages of life).

Svarūpa Dāmodara and Caitanya Mahāprabhu told all philosophical truths regarding *bhakti* to Raghunātha dāsa when he came to them, and in this way he became both learned and

17 See Endnote 7, at the end of this chapter.

renounced. He was so renounced that he used to eat the old, rotting food remnants of Lord Jagannātha that were rejected even by the cows. Let us become qualified like this, and then we will be qualified for the eleven kinds of moods. And then, by our *siddha-deha*, we will be able to serve Śrī Śrī Rādhā and Kṛṣṇa twenty-four hours a day. This is the real method; this is *siddha-praṇālī*.

On the other hand, a bogus *sahajiyā guru* indiscriminately tells his disciple, "You are the daughter of Vṛṣabhānu Mahārāja and you are married in Jāvaṭa. Your place is at Rādhā-kuṇḍa, you are more beautiful than Mohinī, and you are of golden complexion." He thus inspires that disciple to relinquish his big beard and don a nose ring, braid, ladies' ornaments, and ankle bells on his feet. In this disguise, that disciple bears children with many widows.

If externally one has male features and the mood of a male within his heart, but hides this and dresses as a female and associates with ladies, what will happen? Falling further and further into the depths of depravity, he must go to hell, and he is already going.[18] Such disciples consider that they have taken *siddha-praṇālī*. Actually, theirs is not *siddha-praṇālī* – *siddha* meaning 'perfect' and *praṇālī* meaning 'process' or 'system' – but *asiddha-praṇālī*, the process of imperfection.

At our present stage we will have to remember all our *anarthas*, our impure thoughts and habits, and our *aparādhas*, or offenses. We all have a constitutional spiritual form, but it is hidden within our gross and subtle body by Śrī Kṛṣṇa's deluding material potency known as *māyā*. It is there, but who is qualified to realize it? Have the *bābājīs* written any book regarding the method for becoming qualified to realize our spiritual forms? Never. In fact, they don't know any philosophy.

---

18 See Endnote 8, at the end of this chapter.

Once, our Guru Mahārāja was in Vṛndāvana doing Vraja-maṇḍala *parikramā* (the circumambulation of the holy land of Vraja) with about four hundred pilgrims. He invited many *bābājīs* and hundreds gathered there. Guru Mahārāja questioned all the *sahajiyā bābājīs*, "What is the aim and object of your *sādhana* (spiritual practices) and *bhajana*?" They replied, "We want to be liberated; we want to merge into *brahma* (the impersonal Absolute); we want to become *brahma*." They were ignorant of the fact that this is *māyāvāda* philosophy, the doctrine of illusion and impersonalism, which is quite against *bhakti*. Hearing their replies, Guru Mahārāja became both sad and angry, and he began to defeat all their arguments.

We should know that our *guru-paramparā* is bona fide. Don't associate with these *bābājīs* unless you are strong like us. I used to go to Rādhā-kuṇḍa during *parikramā* time and challenge them, "If you are learned, if you know any philosophical conclusive truths from *śāstra*, then come and discuss these topics with me. If I am defeated I will become a *bābājī* and I will be your disciple; otherwise, you must become my disciple." None of them came to meet my challenge.

Have you read *Jaiva-dharma*? Try to read it very carefully. There, we read about two persons, Vijaya Kumāra and Vrajanātha. At first, in Māyāpura, these devotees accepted Premadāsa Bābājī as their *guru* from whom they learned the sixty-four kinds of *bhakti*. Then, when they became expert, their *guru* sent them to Jagannātha Purī to meet with Gopāla Guru Gosvāmī. From Gopāla Guru Gosvāmī they learned the difference between *bhakti* and *bhakti-rasa*, and how *bhakti* can turn into *bhakti-rasa*.[19] They learned deeply and perfectly

---

19 The entire process of *bhakti* encompasses the beginning stages to the most advanced stages. *Bhakti-rasa* is defined as the mellow of one's particular relationship with Kṛṣṇa. It occurs only when the devotee's permanent mood, or *sthāyībhāva*, mixes in... (Continued on the next page)

about the identity of Kṛṣṇa, Śrīmatī Rādhikā, and the *gopīs*. It was not until after this that Gopāla Guru Gosvāmī gave them the *ekādaśa* (eleven) moods and *ḍor-kaupīna*. This is the process, or *siddha-praṇālī*.

Śrīla Bhaktivinoda Ṭhākura teaches that a *guru* should consider to whom he is going to give *bābājī-veśa*; whether or not such recipients have given up attraction to money. He considers whether they have renounced their attachment to the tongue in the form of taking *bīḍīs*, cigarettes, wine, *gāñjā* (marijuana), *gāñjā-bhāṇga* (a drink made from marijuana), and other drugs, as these untouchable substances certainly lead them to degraded lower realms, to hell. Some Indian *yogīs* consider that their spiritual life and *yoga* practice will be helped by taking *gāñjā-bhāṇga*. They think, "Now we are absorbed in *kṛṣṇa-prema*." They are so foolish; they cannot imagine that they are going to become mad like dogs and hogs.

These detestable things have been condemned in the books of Śrīla Rūpa Gosvāmī and Śrīla Jīva Gosvāmī, in *Śrī Caitanya-caritāmṛta*, and in *Śrīmad-Bhāgavatam*. *Śrīmad-Bhāgavatam* (1.17.38) states:

sūta uvāca
abhyarthitas tadā tasmai
sthānāni kalaye dadau
dyūtaṁ pānaṁ striyaḥ sūnā
yatrādharmaś catur-vidhaḥ

[Sūta Gosvāmī said: "Mahārāja Parīkṣit, thus being petitioned by the personality of Kali, gave him permission to reside in places where gambling, drinking, prostitution, and animal slaughter were performed."*]

...correct proportions with the appropriate ingredients – *vibhāva, anubhāva, sāttvika-bhāva*, and *sañcārī-bhāva* (see pages 20–22) – to give the devotee the taste, or mellow, of his direct service to Kṛṣṇa –Ed.

Avoidance of these basic prohibited activities is not *bhakti* in and of itself, but it will take us to the door of *bhakti*. *Dyūtaṁ* means 'gambling,' *pānaṁ* means 'intoxication in the form of cigarettes, *bīḍīs*, tobacco, the *masālā* of tobacco, and marijuana,' all of which surely bring lust in a day or two, or three. The intelligence of such persons who take these intoxications disappears, and they leave the path of *bhakti*; that is sure. Here in the First Canto of *Śrīmad-Bhāgavatam*, Śrī Śukadeva Gosvāmī has prohibited the taking of all these intoxicants for all kinds of devotees.

In India, some so-called Vaiṣṇavas of Rāmānandī take opium, *gāñjā*, *pān*, and very big water pipes, imagining that the high flame of their water pipe indicates their exalted Vaiṣṇava status. Moreover, in their dangerous condition of being in the mode of ignorance, they become naked and quarrel with each other. Try to avoid this *mahā-mahā* poison.

Śrīla Bhaktivinoda Ṭhākura explains in *Jaiva-dharma* that if one has any desire for making money or for sense gratification, he should not take the dress of a renunciant.[20] Similarly, Śrīla Rūpa Gosvāmī tells us in *Śrī Upadeśāmṛta* (Verse 1):

vāco vegaṁ manasaḥ krodha-vegaṁ
jihvā-vegam udaropastha-vegam
etān vegān yo viṣaheta dhīraḥ
sarvām apīmāṁ pṛthivīṁ sa śiṣyāt

> [A wise and self-composed person who can subdue the impetus to speak, the agitation of the mind, the onset of anger, the vehemence of the tongue, the urge of the belly and the agitation of the genitals can instruct the entire world. In other words, all persons may become disciples of such a self-controlled person.]

If one who is not in this stage is given *siddha-praṇālī*, then it is not *siddha-praṇālī*; it is the *praṇālī*, or process, to go to hell.

20 See Endnote 9, at the end of this chapter.

We must endeavor to be very strong in following our *guru-paramparā*. Our *guru-paramparā* is right, and their so-called *guru-paramparā* is artificial. Their so-called *siddha-praṇālī* is only about one hundred years old, whereas our real *siddha-praṇālī* has come from the ancient Vedas and Upaniṣads. We see that Śaṅkara (Lord Śiva) gave *siddha-praṇālī* to the four Kumāras, and Nārada gave it to other qualified devotees. We certainly accept the concept of *siddha-praṇālī*, but in the right process and at the right time.

There are some groups in Vṛndāvana whose followers say that Śrīla Bhaktisiddhānta Sarasvatī Ṭhākura has no *siddha-praṇālī* and no *guru-paramparā*, just as they say that Śrīla Bhaktivinoda Ṭhākura has no *guru-paramparā*. We must think about this very deeply and carefully.

Who was the *guru* of Parīkṣit Mahārāja? We know that he had a family *guru*, a priest, someone like Śāṇḍilya Ṛṣi, but he heard *Śrīmad-Bhāgavatam* from Śrīla Śukadeva Gosvāmī, who was a fully self-realized Vaiṣṇava. He was renounced, detached from worldly desires, quite free, and he had been given all realizations from his father and *guru*, Śrīla Vyāsadeva (the literary incarnation of Kṛṣṇa and manifester of all the Vedic scriptures). Parīkṣit Mahārāja heard *Śrīmad-Bhāgavatam* from him, and as a result of such hearing – not even practicing – he went directly to Goloka Vṛndāvana. Moreover, Śrīla Sanātana Gosvāmī has explained in *Bṛhad-bhāgavatāmṛta* that Parīkṣit Mahārāja became a *gopī* in the service of Śrī Śrī Rādhā and Kṛṣṇa. This is the real process.

True Guru is Eternal

Śrīla Bhaktivinoda Ṭhākura and Śrīla Bhaktisiddhānta Sarasvatī Ṭhākura are bona fide disciples of Jagannātha dāsa Bābājī Mahārāja and Śrīla Gaura Kiśora dāsa Bābājī Mahārāja respectively. Someone may say, "Where is Śrīla Bhaktisiddhānta

Sarasvatī Ṭhākura's *siddha-praṇālī*?" Our reply is that he heard all appropriate topics from his *śikṣā-guru* and father, Śrīla Bhaktivinoda Ṭhākura, as Parīkṣit Mahārāja heard everything from Śrīla Śukadeva Gosvāmī.

Actually, there are two processes.[21] In one process, if a devotee is qualified in all *bhakti* principles, as were Vijaya Kumāra in *Jaiva-dharma* or Parīkṣit Mahārāja in the *Śrīmad-Bhāgavatam*, he can minimize his dress and take *ḍor* and *kaupīna* himself; there is nothing wrong in this.

For example, Rāmānuja took initiation from a *guru* of low caste who was a disciple of Yamunācārya, and later Rāmānuja wanted to take the renounced order from Yamunācārya himself. When he reached Śrī Raṅgam, he saw that Yamunācārya had just left this world, and his divine body was coming in procession for being given *samādhi*[22]. He saw that three fingers of Yamunācārya's hand were closed. He asked some other disciples of Yamunācārya why this was so, but they could not answer. He then promised, "I will take *sannyāsa* here, from him. Just now I am taking *sannyāsa*." And at that moment one of his *gurudeva's* fingers relaxed and opened. Then he promised, "I will write a commentary on Vedānta." The second finger became relaxed. Then he promised, "I will preach pure *bhakti* and I will write many *bhakti* books," and at once the third finger relaxed and opened. He thus accepted Yamunācārya as his *sannyāsa-guru*, knowing, "My *gurudeva* did not die; he is eternal."

A bona fide, qualified *guru* never dies. You can know that your Prabhupāda, Śrīla Bhaktivedānta Svāmī Mahārāja, has not died, and Śrīla Prabhupāda Bhaktisiddhānta Sarasvatī Ṭhākura has also not died.[23] Thus Rāmānuja took *sannyāsa*

---

21 See Endnote 10, at the end of this chapter.

22 A *samādhi* is the tomb in which a pure Vaiṣṇava's body is laid after his departure from this world –Ed.

23 See Endnote 11, at the end of this chapter.

from Yamunācārya after Yamunācārya's departure from this world. Similarly, why can't Śrīla Prabhupāda Bhaktisiddhānta Sarasvatī Ṭhākura take the renounced order from Gaura Kiśora dāsa Bābājī Mahārāja, from his photo, after his departure? Śrīla Gaura Kiśora dāsa Bābājī Mahārāja had disappeared from the world's vision by that time, but he is eternal. And Śrīla Prabhupāda took the *siddha-praṇālī*, *ekādaśa* moods (the eleven moods), and *siddha-deha*, from Śrīla Bhaktivinoda Ṭhākura. This is not wrong; it is in the line of *guru-paramparā*.

No one can deny this. If we cannot deny Śukadeva Gosvāmī, Sanātana Gosvāmī, Rūpa Gosvāmī, Vyāsadeva, Rāmānuja, and Madhvācārya, then we cannot deny Śrīla Prabhupāda Bhaktisiddhānta Sarasvatī Ṭhākura.

Śrīla Prabhupāda was so bold. He was *jagad-guru*. Following in the line of Śrīla Bhaktivinoda Ṭhākura, he brought about revolutionary transformation in the Gauḍīya Vaiṣṇava *sampradāya* and restored its lost dignity. He is certainly in *guru-paramparā*.

[When Śrīla Bhaktisiddhānta Sarasvatī Ṭhākura saw that many *bābājīs* were now bogus, that they were with widow *mātājīs* and producing sons, he became furious and said that we will again accept the same saffron cloth of those like Rāmānujācārya, Madhvācārya, Mahāprabhu, and Īśvara Purīpāda. He then preached everywhere in the world.

At that time, those family persons who were of loose character and had no status in society honored these bogus *bābājīs*. That is why he re-introduced the reddish cloth and *sannyāsa*.][24]

Regarding Śrīla Bhaktivinoda Ṭhākura, he took all his moods from Jagannātha dāsa Bābājī Mahārāja, and that is why he was able to write down the correct understanding of *siddha-praṇālī*, which descends in the heart of pure devotees in the stage of *bhāva*.

---

24 This insertion is an excerpt from a lecture by Śrīla Bhaktivedānta Nārāyaṇa Gosvāmī Mahārāja, spoken in Holland on June 10, 2001.

I know so many persons who left Śrīla Bhaktivedānta Svāmī Mahārāja and went to those *bābājīs*. They returned to their lusty activities, taking so many *mātājīs* here and there, and leaving every aspect of *bhakti*. Now they are drinking, making merry, taking drugs, and engaging in other abominable activities. I am aware that one of them has even committed suicide. I have served all the main disciples of Śrīla Bhaktisiddhānta Sarasvatī Ṭhākura, and I associated with all of them. I therefore know so many things that most devotees don't know. Those who are bewildered in this regard will taste the bitter fruits of their bewilderment.

Endnotes

1 An excerpt from *Ācārya Kesarī Śrī Śrīmad Bhakti Prajñāna Keśava Gosvāmī – His Life and Teachings*, Part Six:

Some ignorant people say that there is no *siddha-praṇālī* in the Gauḍīya Maṭha. This vicious propaganda is erroneous in all respects. In the authentic literatures written by Śrīla Gopāla Bhaṭṭa Gosvāmī entitled *Sat-kriyā-sāra-dīpikā* and *Saṁskāra-dīpikā*, which is a supplement to *Hari-bhakti-vilāsa*, there is an account of the *tridaṇḍi sannyāsa saṁskāra*. The original manuscript handwritten by Śrī Gopāla Bhaṭṭa Gosvāmī is protected even today in the Royal Library of Jaipura, and the *gosvāmīs* of Śrī Rādhā-Ramaṇa still have an old copy of it. Therefore, *Sat-kriyā-sāra-dīpikā* and *Saṁskāra-dīpikā* are accepted as authoritative evidence, and according to them, the conferring of *tridaṇḍi sannyāsa veśa* (the dress of a *sannyāsī*, renunciate) by Gauḍīyas Vaiṣṇavas is bona fide. In this *sannyāsa saṁskāra* (the ceremony of awarding *sannyāsa*) *ḍor-kaupīna* (loin cloth), *bahir-vāsa* (outer garments) and the *sannyāsa-mantra* for taking shelter of *gopī-bhāva* (the mood of devotion for Śrī Kṛṣṇa possessed by the cowherd women of Vraja) are given. The *ekādaśa-bhāva* (eleven aspects of *gopī* identity), namely *sambandha, vayaḥ, nāma, rūpa, yūtha, veśa, ājñā, vāsa, sevā, parākāṣṭā-śvāsa,* and *pālya-dāsī-bhāva,*[25] are contained within *gopī-bhāva*. The identity of the *siddha-deha* is determined by the instructions of *śrī guru* in accordance with the *ruci* (taste) of the *sādhaka* (devotional practitioner). One's own eleven identifications (*ekādaśa-bhāva*) given by *guru* are called *siddha-praṇālī*. As the *sādhaka* goes on performing this type of *sādhana*, the perfection of his *svarūpa* (constitutional spiritual form) takes place along with the attainment of *śuddha-rati* (pure attachment for Śrī Śrī Rādhā-Kṛṣṇa) in his heart.

2 There is another, much more rare and quite bona fide meaning of '*bābājī* initiation.' In our Gauḍīya Maṭha line, *bābājī* initiation is the same as *sannyāsa* initiation, except that the color of the cloth is white (instead of the saffron cloth of *sannyāsa*, the renounced order), and the devotee is primarily focused upon chanting *harināma* and rendering service to Ṭhākurajī (Deity worship). There is no emphasis upon outward preaching service. In that regard, Śrīla Nārāyaṇa Gosvāmī Mahārāja gave *bābājī* initiation to three or four disciples, and his *guru mahārāja*, Śrīla Bhakti Prajñāna Keśava Gosvāmī Mahārāja, gave such initiation to about ten disciples –Ed.

3 An excerpt from a *darśana* with Śrīla Bhaktivedānta Nārāyaṇa Gosvāmī Mahārāja in France on April 27, 1999:

Śrīla Nārāyaṇa Gosvāmī Mahārāja: I have written a very good essay on this subject (in Hindi). I want it to be translated in the form of a booklet as soon as possible.

Jayanta-kṛṣṇa dāsa (later to become Śrīpāda Śuddhādvaitī Mahārāja): Yes, there should be a publication. There is so much

---

25 These terms are more elaborately explained on pages 5–6.

confusion at present. They say that the *bābājīs* quote Sanātana Gosvāmī, just as we do.

Śrīla Nārāyaṇa Gosvāmī Mahārāja: That is not possible. Sanātana Gosvāmī was not *bābājī*. From where do they say he took *bābājī* initiation?

Jayanta-kṛṣṇa dāsa: They are not saying that. They say that they are quoting his teachings. They say, "We are coming from Sanātana Gosvāmī."

Śrīla Nārāyaṇa Gosvāmī Mahārāja: Never, never, never. Where is that line of succession? There is no teaching of his that they can quote. From whom do they say Sanātana Gosvāmī took *bābājī-veśa*?

Brajanāth dāsa: They are not telling about that. They are just quoting his teachings.

Śrīla Nārāyaṇa Gosvāmī Mahārāja: Why are they not telling this? They should tell from whom Sanātana Gosvāmī took *bābājī-veśa*. Do they quote any reference? Is it written anywhere? Actually, he took some old cloth from Tapāna Miśra and made his own garments. There was no *mantra* given to him; nothing of the sort.

Jayanta-kṛṣṇa dāsa: So where is this *siddha-praṇālī* coming from?

Śrīla Nārāyaṇa Gosvāmī Mahārāja: *Siddha-praṇālī* is coming from the very beginning. It is discussed in our scriptures. But it is not like what they say.

Jayanta-kṛṣṇa dāsa: No *ekādaśa-bhāva* (the eleven aspects of *gopī bhāva*)?

Śrīla Nārāyaṇa Gosvāmī Mahārāja: *Ekādaśa-bhāva* is bona fide, but it will come at the stage of *bhāva-bhakti*. First comes *āsakti*, and then *bhāva*, and at that time it will come through the mercy of the bona fide *paramparā*. It will descend from the heart of the *rāgātmikā* associate of the Lord and manifest in the heart of the disciple. It will not come by taking any special *mantra* from others. That is why they are all characterless, bogus persons.

Śrīla Bhaktivinoda Ṭhākura has stated in *Jaiva-dharma* and in his songs that it will come by the mercy of Śrīmatī Rādhikā, in the higher stage. Not that a *guru* would give *ekādaśa-bhāvas* to someone who does not know anything about proper *siddhānta* (philosophical conclusion) or proper behavior, and who does not even clean himself after passing stool and urine. They want *mokṣa*, liberation. They think, "By practicing in this way we will have liberation. We will mix with Kṛṣṇa."

Jayanta-kṛṣṇa dāsa: Merging.

Brajanāth dāsa: *Nikuñja-sevā*.

Śrīla Nārāyaṇa Gosvāmī Mahārāja: Why *nikuñja-sevā*?

Brajanāth dāsa: They think that they will attain *nikuñja-sevā*, where Rādhā-Kṛṣṇa are always one.

Śrīla Nārāyaṇa Gosvāmī Mahārāja: No, no. They think that they will merge in *brahma* (the impersonal absolute). They think, "After doing all this *bhakti* – chanting *harināma* and hearing *harināma* if we become *siddha*, pure, we will merge in *brahma* and become *brahma*." There are so many *bābājīs* like this, and they give their conception of *ekādaśa-bhāva* to other persons who think like this. Where is the origin of giving this? Did Caitanya Mahāprabhu give this? Who is the originator? They cannot say. They have no *paramparā*, but we have *paramparā*.

Jayanta-kṛṣṇa dāsa: Sometimes they say that they are coming from the Gadādhara line, or the Advaita line.

Śrīla Nārāyaṇa Gosvāmī Mahārāja: Did Nityānanda Prabhu take *ekādaśa-bhāva* from any *bābājī*? Never. Was there even any such *bābājī* at that time? Who created *bābājī*? Can anyone show this *bābājī* line, or even the name *bābājī*, in *Śrī Caitanya-caritāmṛta*? It is not there.

Rather, Śrī Caitanya Mahāprabhu told Raghunātha dāsa Gosvāmī:[26]

antare niṣṭhā kara bāhye loka-vyavahāra
acirāt kṛṣṇa tomāya karibe uddhāra
(*Śrī Caitanya-caritāmṛta, Madhya-līlā* 16.239)

mane' nija-siddha-deha kariyā bhāvana
rātri-dine kare vraje kṛṣṇera sevana
(*Śrī Caitanya-caritāmṛta, Madhya-līlā* 22.152)

This is *siddha-praṇālī*. And also:

tṛṇād api sunīcena
taror api sahiṣṇunā
amāninā mānadena
kīrtanīyaḥ sadā hariḥ
(*Śikṣāṣṭaka* 3)

[Thinking oneself to be even lower and more worthless than insignificant grass that has been trampled beneath everyone's feet, being more tolerant than a

26 These two verses are explained as follows in *Ācārya Kesarī Śrī Śrīmad Bhakti Prajñāna Keśava Gosvāmī – His Life and Teachings*, Part Six:

"Here Śrī Caitanya Mahāprabhujī is saying that in the beginning one's *niṣṭhā*, firm faith, is to be kept within the core of one's heart, and at the same time one is to behave like an ordinary person in order to sustain one's life. Gradually, when one's faith becomes mature, his worldly activities will also come to correspond with his *bhajana*; that is, they will become favorable to *bhajana*. In such a condition, one should meditate on one's internally conceived *siddha-deha* suitable for the service of the Divine Couple, and in the core of one's heart one should mentally serve Them (*aprākṛta mānasī-sevā*). By following this procedure, at first one attains *svarūpa-siddhi*, realization of one's eternal spiritual body. Ultimately, at the stage of *vastu-siddhi* (the spiritual body one receives upon attaining *prema* and taking birth in Vraja) in *prakaṭa* Vraja (the spiritual realm of Vraja which manifests in this world), after giving up the material body, one receives the body of a *gopī* corresponding to one's internally conceived *siddha-deha*."

tree, being prideless and offering respect to all others according to their respective positions, one should continuously chant the holy name of Śrī Hari.]

Western devotees are becoming influenced by them, more than before. Mad and lusty men and women fall in the trap of such *bābājīs*. They don't want to follow books like *Upadeṣāmṛta* or *Manaḥ-śikṣā*. They don't know whether or not there are such books.

4 An excerpt from *Five Essential Essays*, Addendum Two :

After Śrīman Mahāprabhu, His eternal pastime associates such as the six Gosvāmīs, Śrī Lokanātha, and Śrī Bhūgarbha, and later Śrī Kṛṣṇadāsa Kavirāja, Śrī Narottama Ṭhākura, and Śrī Viśvanātha Cakravartī Ṭhākura were naturally *niṣkiñcana, paramahāṁsa* Vaiṣṇavas. There was no need for them to wear *sannyāsa-veśa*, saffron cloth. Secondly, Śrīman Mahāprabhu had performed the pastime of wearing *sannyāsa-veśa* and saffron cloth.

Thus considering themselves to be worthless, lowly, and unqualified, these *mahātmās* did not wear *sannyāsa-veśa* and saffron cloth, in order to show honor and respect to the *veśa* of Śrīman Mahāprabhu and also to maintain their own identities as servants under the shelter of His lotus feet.

On the other hand, in order to express veneration for the *niṣkiñcana paramahāṁsa-veśa* of the associates of Śrīman Mahāprabhu and, under their guidance to preach His message throughout the entire world, many *akiñcana* Vaiṣṇavas on the path of *rāgānuga-bhajana*, holding the *paramahāṁsa-veśa* upon their heads, have accepted a position below their worshipable superiors by wearing the saffron cloth of the *sannyāsa āśrama* (the renounced order), which is included within the system of *varṇāśrama dharma* (the Vedic system for the organization of civilized society).

These two customs, each having their own place, are both exquisitely beautiful and also completely in accordance with *siddhānta*. Today *śuddha-hari-bhakti* has been, is being, and will continue to be, preached and spread throughout the world by these *mahāpuruṣas*, great perfected saints, who wear this second type of *niṣkiñcana sannyāsī-veśa*.

5 An excerpt from *Ācārya Kesarī Śrī Śrīmad Bhakti Prajñāna Keśava Gosvāmī – His Life and Teachings*, Part Four:

The system of *bhāgavata-paramparā* is superior to that of *pāñcarātrika-paramparā*, and is founded on the degree of proficiency in *bhajana* (*bhajana-niṣṭhā*). The charm and superiority of *bhāgavata-paramparā* is that *pāñcarātrika-paramparā* is included within it. In *bhāgavata-paramparā* there is no obstruction in regard to time. From the viewpoint of pure *bhakti*, the doctrines of *pāñcarātrika* and of *bhāgavata* both explain the same teachings with the same objective. In *Śrī Caitanya-caritāmṛta* (*Madhya-līlā* 19.169) it is said, "*pañcarātra bhāgavate ei lakṣana kaya* – these symptoms are described in Vedic literatures such as the Pañcarātras and *Śrīmad-Bhāgavatam*".

The *prākṛta-sahajiyā sampradāya*, while claiming to be followers of Śrī Rūpa Gosvāmī, accumulate offenses to the lotus feet of Śrī Jīva Gosvāmī. Similarly, nowadays the *jāti-gosvāmīs* and those who accept their remnants – such as several members of the *sahajiyā*, *kartābhajā*, *kiśorībhajā*, and *bhajanākhājā sampradāyas* – proudly conceive of themselves as followers of Cakravartī Ṭhākura, but cast calumnies against the commentator Śrī Baladeva Vidyābhūṣaṇa (who is Śrīla Cakravartī Ṭhākura's main disciple and successor). In this way, they are growing excessively hateful and progressing towards hell.

[...] Several additional facts are worthy of our consideration on the subject of *pāñcarātrika-guru-paramparā* and *bhāgavata-paramparā*:

(1) *The guru of lower rasa*: If a *pāñcarātrika-dīkṣā-guru* in his constitutional spiritual form (*siddha-svarūpa*) is situated in a *rasa* that is lower than that of his disciple, how can he give *bhajana-śikṣā* (instructions on how to perform ones spiritual practices) pertaining to the more elevated *rasa*? In this situation, the disciple must go elsewhere and take shelter of a Vaiṣṇava who is qualified to give the appropriate superior guidance. For example, Śrī Hṛdaya Caitanya is an associate in *sakhya-rasa* (attachment for Kṛṣṇa in the mood of a friend) in *kṛṣṇa-līlā* (Śrī Kṛṣṇa's pastimes), whereas his disciple Śrī Śyāmānanda Prabhu (Duḥkhi Kṛṣṇa dāsa) is an associate in *madhura-rasa* (conjugal love). Therefore Śrī Hṛdaya Caitanya personally sent Duḥkhi Kṛṣṇa dāsa to Śrīla Jīva Gosvāmī to receive higher *bhajana-śikṣā* in *madhura-rasa*.

(2) *The less qualified guru*: It may happen that *guru* and disciple in *pāñcarātrika-guru-paramparā* are in the same *rasa*, but that the *guru* is not so highly qualified as the disciple. Under such circumstances, the disciple must go and take shelter of an *uttama* (topmost) Vaiṣṇava for higher *bhajana-śikṣā*, and this Vaiṣṇava will be called his *guru* in the *bhāgavata-paramparā*.

We can see from these two considerations that the *pāñcarātrika* process has some inherent defects, whereas the *bhāgavata-paramparā* is completely free from these defects and is flawless in all respects.

(3) *Śrīman Mahāprabhu is not pāñcarātrika-guru of anyone*: All members of the Gauḍīya-*sampradāya* accept Śrī Caitanya Mahāprabhu as *jagad-guru* and consider themselves to be His followers. However, on what basis do they maintain this conviction? There is no recorded account anywhere of Śrīman Mahāprabhu giving *dīkṣā-mantra* (the *mantras* given by the *guru* at the time of initiation) to anyone. This means that Śrīman Mahāprabhu is not anyone's *guru* in the *pāñcarātrika-paramparā*, although He Himself is a disciple of Śrī Īśvara Purī.

Therefore, if the Gauḍīya Vaiṣṇava community accepts the guidance and discipleship of Śrī Caitanya Mahāprabhu, it can only be on one basis, and that basis is *bhāgavata-paramparā*.

(4) *All Gauḍīya Vaiṣṇavas are rūpānuga (followers of Śrīla Rūpa Gosvāmī) on the basis of bhāgavata-paramparā only*: Each and every Gauḍīya Vaiṣṇava is proud to call himself *rūpānuga*. But the point to consider is this: how many disciples did Śrī Rūpa Gosvāmī initiate by the *pāñcarātrika* method? The fact is that Śrī Jīva Gosvāmī is his one and only *dīkṣā* disciple, and Śrī Rūpa is not actually a *dīkṣā* disciple of Śrī Caitanya Mahāprabhu. So on what basis do members of the Gauḍīya Vaiṣṇava community accept Śrī Rūpa Gosvāmī as their *guru*? How is it possible to be a follower of Śrī Rūpa Gosvāmī and at the same time be a follower of Śrī Caitanya Mahāprabhu? Even Śrī Sanātana Gosvāmī, who is the *śikṣā-guru* (instructing spiritual master) of Śrī Rūpa Gosvāmī, has not a second thought about calling himself *rūpānuga*. The basis of all these examples is one – *bhāgavata-paramparā*.

[...] Who is the *pāñcarātrika-dīkṣā-guru* of Śrīla Kṛṣṇadāsa Kavirāja Gosvāmī? We cannot say, because he has not mentioned the name of his *pāñcarātrika-dīkṣā-guru* in any of his writings, but he has named his *śikṣā-gurus* in *Śrī Caitanya-caritāmṛta* (*Ādi-līlā* 1.37): "These six *gurus* (the six Gosvāmīs of Vṛndāvana) are my *śikṣā-gurus* and I offer countless obeisances at their lotus feet." At the end of each chapter of *Śrī Caitanya-caritāmṛta* he has written, "*śrī-rupa-raghunātha-pade yāra āśa, caitanya caritāmṛta kahe kṛṣṇa dāsa* – Praying at the lotus feet of Śrī Rūpa and Śrī Raghunātha, always desiring their mercy, I, Kṛṣṇadāsa, narrate *Śrī Caitanya-caritāmṛta*, following in their footsteps."* In these statements he has specifically accepted Śrī Rūpa Gosvāmī and Śrī Raghunātha dāsa Gosvāmī as his *śikṣā-gurus* on the basis of *bhāgavata guru-paramparā*.

From these facts it becomes thoroughly obvious that *bhāgavata-paramparā*, which includes *pāñcarātrika-paramparā*, always shines forth brilliantly.

6 An excerpt from *Ācārya Kesarī Śrī Śrīmad Bhakti Prajñāna Keśava Gosvāmī – His Life and Teachings*, Part Six:

There is a terrible and disastrous custom among *bābājīs* of keeping maidservants in their *āśramas*. In some *āśramas*, a *bābājī* may even keep his former wife as his maidservant. These people associate with women on the pretext of serving God and the *sādhus*.

7 An excerpt from a lecture by Śrīla Bhaktivedānta Nārāyaṇa Gosvāmī Mahārāja in Oahu, Hawaii, on January 18, 2002:

From *niṣṭhā*, *ruci*, or taste, manifests. This taste is divided into two: *vastu-vaiśiṣṭya apekṣaṇī* and *vastu-vaiśiṣṭya anapekṣaṇī*. After passing the stage at which many *anarthas* remain, this taste may arise. Some *anarthas* are still there, but not *nāma-aparādha*. The *anarthas* of the devotee in the stage of *ruci* are now in a very minute form.

An example of *apekṣaṇī-ruci* is as follows: When someone sings with a guitar, with harmonium, with so many instruments, and with a very sweet melody and voice, it will be very tasteful. On the other hand, if a high-class devotee, weeping with a melting heart, is singing with no instrument, and his voice is not so sweet, then that hearer will not have taste to hear. If that devotee sees that any deities are well-dressed, he will have taste in Their *darśana*, and if the same deities not well-dressed, no taste will occur.

[...] When *ruci* first develops, it depends on good melody, good decoration, and so on. When it further develops, the devotee is more advanced, and Śrīmatī Rādhikā is an example of that. She is far superior to *ruci*, but I am giving an example. Once Śrīmatī Rādhikā heard someone talking about Kṛṣṇa from very far away and She fainted. In this way there are two classes of *ruci*. Then, as *ruci* continues through its most complete stage of *vastu-vaiśiṣṭya anapekṣaṇī*, it will be then changed into *āsakti*.

8 An excerpt from *Ācārya Kesarī Śrī Śrīmad Bhakti Prajñāna Keśava Gosvāmī – His Life and Teachings*, Part Six:

Others do not adorn their male bodies in the dress of women, but they support the conception of those who do. With flirtatious gestures, they indiscriminately sing about the confidential loving play of Rāī-Kānū (Rādhā-Kṛṣṇa) in the presence of any ordinary people in the marketplace, without considering the eligibility of their audience. They give pretentious lectures on *rāsa-līlā* and imitate it. Thus these debauchees cheapen the *aprākṛta-rasa* (supramundane mellows) for the *jaḍa* (material) *rasa*. They believe that it is absolutely necessary to keep the company of another's wife as an illicit paramour in order to realize *aprākṛta-rasa*. Conversely, they think that Śrī Jīva Gosvāmī and Śrīla Narottama Ṭhākura cannot possibly be *rasika*, because Śrī Jīva Gosvāmī was a *brahmacārī* from boyhood and Śrīla Narottama Ṭhākura never entered household life. Such people, also, come in the category of *prākṛta-sahajiyā*.

9 An excerpt from *Jaiva-dharma*, Chapter 7:

Yādava dāsa: Who can give *veśa* [initiation into the renounced order, along with the dress of a renunciant]?

Ananta dāsa Bābājī: One should receive *veśa* from a *gṛha-tyāgī* (renunciant) *bhakta*. A *gṛhastha-bhakta* has not experienced the life of a renunciant; hence, he must not give *veśa* to anybody. The *Brahma-vaivarta Purāṇa* states: "*aparīkṣyopadiṣṭaṁ yat loka-nāśāya tad bhavet* – Without first practicing spiritual life, one should not advise others, as this will create chaos in society."

Yādava dāsa: What are the points a *guru* must consider when he initiates a devotee with *veśa*?

Ananta dāsa Bābājī: The first point a *guru* must consider is whether the disciple is competent. Has he, as a *gṛhastha-bhakta* (householder devotee), been able to attain the brahminical qualities such as equanimity, sense control, and so on by practicing devotional service to Kṛṣṇa? Has he shaken off the desire to associate with women? Has he uprooted the material cravings for wealth, opulent food and clothing, and luxurious living? The *guru* will have the disciple stay with him for some time to test him properly. Only when he is convinced of his disciple's eligibility, and not before, will he initiate him into *veśa*. The *guru* will surely fall down if he initiates an undeserving disciple.

Yādava dāsa: Now I understand that receiving *veśa* is not an easy affair, but is actually an extremely serious observance. Indeed, the unqualified, so-called *gurus* have made this *veśa* a mere meaningless ritual, a farce. Unfortunately this is only the beginning. I wonder where all this will end?

Ananta dāsa Bābājī: It was in order to protect the sanctity of this process that Śrī Caitanya chastised Choṭa Haridāsa for a minor deviation. Those who claim to be followers of my Lord, Śrī Mahāprabhu, must always remember this punishment of Choṭa Haridāsa.

10 An excerpt from *Five Essential Essays*, Chapter 4:

A *sādhaka* may receive *sannyāsa-veśa* (the saffron cloth of the renounced order) from some suitable *guru*; and alternatively, when genuine *vairāgya* (renunciation at the stage of *bhāva-bhakti*) arises, he may accept *veśa* from himself. Haridāsa Ṭhākura, the six Gosvāmīs, Lokanātha Gosvāmī, and others are examples of the practice of accepting *veśa* from oneself. This is also the way Śrīla Bhaktisiddhānta Sarasvatī Ṭhākura accepted *sannyāsa-veśa* after the disappearance of Śrīla Gaura Kiśora dāsa Bābājī, from whom he had received the *dīkṣā-mantra*.

We see from these examples that acceptance of *veśa* in this way is fully in agreement with *śāstra*. Śrī Rāmānujācārya also accepted *tridaṇḍi sannyāsa* from himself after the disappearance of his *guru* Śrīla Yamunācārya.

11 An excerpt from a lecture by Śrīla Bhakti Prajñāna Keśava Gosvāmī Mahārāja, published in *The Rays of The Harmonist*, Issue 25 (Tirobhāva Edition), 2011:[27]

By using the words 'birth' and 'death,' a kind of mournful mood, full of disbelief, grief, and lamentation arises in the heart. But such moods do not arise when we use words like *avirbhāva* and *tirobhāva*, or *prakaṭa* and *aprakaṭa*. Factually, for the Vaiṣṇava, pain is completely absent in his appearance and disappearance, unlike the experience of birth and death. Generally, therefore, the Vaiṣṇavas do not use the term 'birth,' but instead say 'appearance' or 'manifestation.' And in place of the term 'death' they say 'disappearance' or 'has become unmanifest.'

We understand this from a statement from *Śrī Caitanya-bhāgavata*, the scripture describing the pastimes of Śrī Caitanyadeva:

adyāpiha sei līlā kare gaurarāya
kona-kona bhāgyavān dekhibāre pāya

Śrī Caitanya Mahāprabhu is still performing His pastimes to this day, but only a few, very fortunate souls can see them.

---

27 This article is copyrighted under the Creative Commons-Attribution-Share Alike (CC-BY-SA) 3.0 unported license.

From this, we can apprehend that Śrī Caitanyadeva's eternal servants and associates are indeed ever-present. Among us, a few had the good fortune, some time ago, to have the direct audience (*darśana*) of Śrīla Bhaktivinoda Ṭhākura, but because it is not possible to see him at present, a doubt can arise that he is existing eternally. It should be understood, however, that despite the inability of our mundane eyes to perceive him, he is still present to this day. Do not be amazed by this! I am speaking the truth, the complete truth. He is present with us even today! I will endeavor to remove your doubt to some extent with an example.

[...] You have seen how a snake leaves its skin and then slithers away in the same form it had before. Upon seeing the skin, we understand that it belongs to a snake. The skin also tells us the exact shape and size of the snake. Although the snake has discarded its full skin, it has gone off in its complete form somewhere else.

[...] In fact, you are also eternal. You also will not die. You will merely change your body as one changes his cloth. I recall one verse from the *Gītā* on this subject. You are aware of the verse (*Bhagavad-gītā* 2.22): "Just as a person discards his old garments and acquires new ones, similarly the embodied soul gives up old bodies and accepts new ones." Do not consider that this verse, which applies only to conditioned souls, also applies to my subject of discussion. There is no difference between the body and the soul of the eternally liberated *mahā-puruṣas*, so if we apply this verse to them, we will incur an offence. As far as we are concerned, there is a vast difference between our 'cloth' (our body) and us.

In this temple room named *avidyā-haraṇa*, that place where ignorance is totally removed, we are taking *darśana* of the *vigraha* (Deity), or the picture, of Śrīla Ṭhākura's manifest (*prakaṭa*) and unmanifest (*aprakaṭa*) pastimes. That *vigraha* is his beautifully decorated worshipful form (*arcā*).

The picture of him before us is his very *arcā-mūrti*, which is transcendental. This form is not transitory but eternal, and this indeed is his form in the manifest (*prakaṭa*) and unmanifest (*aprakaṭa*) pastimes. If this *mūrti* were not eternal, then we would diligently seek out his eternal *mūrti* and worship that alone. But in fact, this very *mūrti* is established at Śrīla Bhaktivinoda Ṭhākura's place of *samādhi*, and thus is never material, or temporary.

Śrī Nārada (1)

After many years, Nārada left his mortal body. At that same moment his *siddha-deha* manifested, and in that *siddha-deha* he became so powerful that he could travel anywhere in the universe or beyond. (p35)

Guru and Disciple (2)

"Only unto those great souls who have implicit faith in both the Lord and the spiritual master are all the imports of Vedic knowledge automatically revealed" (*Śvetāśvatara Upaniṣad* 6.23). (p94)

Śrīla Raghunātha dāsa Gosvāmī (3)

Svarūpa Dāmodara and Caitanya Mahāprabhu told all philosophical truths regarding *bhakti* to Raghunātha dāsa when he came to them, and in this way he became both learned and renounced. He was so renounced that he used to eat the old, rotting food remnants of Lord Jagannātha that were rejected even by the cows. (p50–51)

Śrīla Jīva Gosvāmī (4)

Śrīla Jīva Gosvāmī was *rūpānuga,* a pure follower of Śrīla Rūpa Gosvāmī. (p75)

Śrīla Viśvanātha Cakravartī Ṭhākura (5)

Following in the footsteps of Śrīla Rūpa Gosvāmī, Śrīla Viśvanātha Cakravartī Ṭhākura composed an abundance of transcendental literature on *bhakti*, thereby establishing in this world the innermost desire of Śrīman Mahāprabhu's heart. (Part IV)

Blessings upon Śrīla Sanātana Gosvāmī (6)

Aware of Śrī Caitanya Mahāprabhu's identity as the Supreme Lord, Śrīla Sanātana Gosvāmī had great honor for His saffron cloth and thought, "I cannot be like Him, I am not so high." Out of reverence he wore a simple white cloth, just to minimize his material necessities, and he used to worship Mahāprabhu's saffron cloth. (p81)

Śrī Śukadeva Gosvāmī (7)

Śrī Śukadeva Gosvāmī is totally renounced. For him there is no difference between the most beautiful naked lady and a piece of dry firewood. He has no interest at all in the affairs of men and women. Yet, that Śukadeva Gosvāmī offers reverential obeisances to *rasa-līlā* and *aṣṭa-kālīya-līlā*. (p89)

Śrī Śrī Rādhā-Kṛṣṇa (8)

We conditioned souls have the eligibility to become *mañjarīs*, young maidservants of Śrīmatī Rādhikā, thus serving Kṛṣṇa through Her. This is not a small attainment. (p90)

Śrī Kṛṣṇa, the Source of all Incarnations (9)

Kṛṣṇa Himself manifested as each of the incarnations. They are all the same Kṛṣṇa, but He is playing the role of being Them. (p91)

Śrī Caitanya Mahāprabhu and Śrīla Rūpa Gosvāmī (10)

Śrī Rūpa Gosvāmī knew the mood of Śrī Caitanya Mahāprabhu, because Mahāprabhu had inspired in his heart the contents of His own heart. (p97)

Śrī Caitanya Mahāprabhu (11)

Śrī Caitanya Mahāprabhu is not only Caitanya Mahāprabhu. He is Śrī Kṛṣṇa Himself, having taken the beauty and internal moods of Śrīmatī Rādhikā. (p98)

Śrī Rūpa Mañjarī (12)

"When the Divine Couple enjoy Their conjugal pastimes, these maidservants are not at all shy. They move freely, without hesitation, even more so than the *prāṇa-preṣṭha-sakhīs* (such as Lalitā and Viśakhā). I take shelter of those maidservants, who have Rūpa Mañjarī as their leader" (*Vraja-vilāsa stava* 38, by Śrīla Raghunātha dāsa Gosvāmī). (Part V)

Śrī Rati Mañjarī (13)

The *rāgānuga-bhakta*, or more specifically, the *rūpānuga-bhakta* will follow the rules and regulations of *bhakti* as Śrīla Raghunātha dāsa Gosvāmī did externally, and internally he will follow the mood of Rati Mañjarī. (p100)

Śrīla Vyāsadeva (14)

Śrīmad-Bhāgavatam is the pure evidence regarding transcendental subjects. The writer, or manifester, of *Śrīmad-Bhāgavatam* is *mahā-muni* Śrīla Vyāsadeva, who is Śrī Kṛṣṇa Himself. (p103)

Śaunaka Ṛṣi and the sages approach Śrī Sūta Gosvāmī (15)

Once, in Naimiṣāraṇya, 88,000 learned and realized scholars gathered to hear from Śrī Sūta Gosvāmī, the disciple of Śrīla Śukadeva Gosvāmī. Śrī Sūta Gosvāmī was a most learned scholar of all Vedic literature and a fully self-realized soul. (p105)

Śrī Śrī Rādhā-Kṛṣṇa and Their Associates (16)

The gist of the matter is that Rādhā-Kṛṣṇa's love-laden *līlā* is so confidential and so full of mysteries that it is imperceptible, even for those in *dāsya-bhāva* and *vātsalya-bhāva*. Only the *sakhīs* are eligible for this. (p116)

Part IV

Counterfeit and Genuine Currency

All That Glitters Is Not Gold

I want to explain something so that you will be very careful. I am receiving questions about the books published by some of the *bābājīs* of Vraja. These *bābājīs* claim that they accept Śrī Caitanya Mahāprabhu, Śrī Nityānanda Prabhu, and Śrī Śrī Rādhā-Kṛṣṇa. They have not written their own books. They refer only to books like *Stava-mālā* by Śrīla Rūpa Gosvāmī, *Stavāvalī* and *Vilāpa-kusumāñjali* by Śrīla Raghunātha dāsa Gosvāmī, *Rādhā-rāsa-sudhanidhi* by Śrī Prabhodānanda Sarasvatī, and other Gosvāmī books. They have taken our Gosvāmīs' explanations, which are in Sanskrit, and they are simply translating them into Bengali. Everything seems to be okay – but you should know the defects of these *bābājīs*. Carefully note down their defects in your hearts and your notebooks.

First of all, they don't accept that the Gauḍīya Vaiṣṇava *sampradāya*, the Gauḍīya line of disciplic succession, is one of the branches of the Brahmā-Madhva-*sampradāya*, although this fact has been clearly explained by Śrī Kavi-karṇapūra,

Śrīla Jīva Gosvāmī, and then by Śrī Baladeva Vidyābhūṣaṇa Prabhu. It has also been explained by Śrīla Bhaktivinoda Ṭhākura, Śrīla Bhaktisiddhānta Sarasvatī Ṭhākura, by my *gurudeva* Śrīla Bhakti Prajñāna Keśava Gosvāmī Mahārāja, and also by Śrīla Bhaktivedānta Svāmī Mahārāja.

Second, they think that Śrī Prabhodānanda Sarasvatī and Prakāśānanda Sarasvatī are the same person, although there is so much difference between them. Will a person of the Rāmānuja *sampradāya* go down to become a *māyāvādī* (one who advocates the doctrine of impersonalism) like Prakāśānanda Sarasvatī, and then again become Prabhodānanda Sarasvatī, who was so exalted that he became the *guru* of Śrīla Gopāla Bhaṭṭa Gosvāmī? This idea is absurd. Prabhodānanda Sarasvatī and Prakāśānanda Sarasvatī were contemporaries. Will the same person go back and forth, from being a Vaiṣṇava in South India to becoming a *māyāvādī*, then again becoming a Vaiṣṇava in Vṛndāvana, and again becoming a *māyāvādī*? Śrīla Bhaktisiddhānta Sarasvatī Ṭhākura has vividly written about this, and great historians and research scholars have also rejected the idea that they are the same person.

Third, they don't give proper honor to Śrīla Jīva Gosvāmī, and this is a very big blunder. This is a vital point. They say that Jīva Gosvāmī is of *svakīya-bhāva*, the conception that Śrī Rādhā-Kṛṣṇa are a married couple. They say that he never supported *parakīya-bhāva*, the conception that in Their human-like pastimes They are paramour lovers, and that he is in fact against *parakīya-bhāva*. They say that in his explanations of *Śrīmad-Bhāgavatam* and *Brahma-saṁhitā*, in his own books like *Gopāla-campū*, and especially in his *Śrī Ujjvala-nīlamaṇi ṭīkā*, he has written against *parakīya-bhāva*. This is their greatest blunder. We don't accept their statements at all.

All in One Line

Śrīla Jīva Gosvāmī was *rūpānuga*, a pure follower of Śrīla Rūpa Gosvāmī[1] who, in his *siddha* form as Śrīmatī Rādhikā's maidservant, is Śrī Rūpa Mañjarī. However, for some devotees who were not very qualified at that time, who were beginners, and who would not be able to accept the purity of *parakīya-bhāva* no matter how carefully it was explained – there were so many like this – he seemed to favor *svakīya-bhāva*.

For some followers, so that they would be able to come at least to *vidhi-mārga* (worship according to the rules and regulations of *Nārada-pañcarātra*), Jīva Gosvāmī wrote as if he was a supporter of *svakīya-rasa*. He wanted that through this they would become qualified and then they would come to appreciate the mood of *parakīya*. For qualified persons he has written that *parakīya-bhāva* is in Vraja and *svakīya-bhāva* is in Dvārakā. He has vividly written this, and he also accepted this. He would never speak against the teachings of Śrīla Rūpa Gosvāmī, Śrīla Sanātana Gosvāmī, and Śrī Caitanya Mahāprabhu. He was a follower of the same root idea of *parakīya-bhāva* as propounded by Rūpa Gosvāmī.

Those ignorant *bābājīs* of Vraja could not reconcile this. They became opposed to Śrīla Jīva Gosvāmī and considered that they were taking the side of Śrīla Viśvanātha Cakravartī Ṭhākura, even though there is no dispute between Jīva Gosvāmī and Viśvanātha Cakravartī Ṭhākura.

Whatever Jīva Gosvāmī wrote for the benefit of those unqualified followers is in the line of *tattva-siddhānta*, conclusive philosophical truth. He wrote that by *tattva* the *gopīs* are *kṛṣṇa-svakīya*.

---

1 Śrīla Jīva Gosvāmī was also the only personality who was accepted as the *dīkṣā* disciple of Śrīla Rūpa Gosvāmī –Ed.

ānanda-cinmaya-rasa-pratibhāvitābhis
tābhir ya eva nija-rūpatayā kalābhiḥ
goloka eva nivasaty akhilātma-bhūto
govindam ādi-puruṣaṁ tam ahaṁ bhajāmi

(*Brahma-saṁhitā* 5.37)

[I worship Govinda, the primeval Lord, who resides in His own realm, Goloka, with Rādhā, who resembles His own spiritual figure and who embodies the ecstatic potency (*hlādinī*). Their companions are Her confidantes, who embody extensions of Her bodily form and who are imbued and permeated with ever-blissful spiritual *rasa*.]

Nija-rūpatayā kalābhiḥ. The *gopīs* are Kṛṣṇa's power. They cannot be *parakīya* in the eyes of *tattva-siddhānta*. They are non-different from Kṛṣṇa, being His power. They are also not the wives of any cowherd men of Vṛndāvana. By *tattva* they are *svakīya*. (*Sva* means 'own' and *kīya* means *sampatti*, or 'wealth.') This means they are of Kṛṣṇa, Kṛṣṇa's own, and they are His power.

Śrīla Viśvanātha Cakravartī Ṭhākura has written in the line of *rasa-tattva*, or pastimes. In *rasa-tattva*, Yogamāyā has arranged that both the *gopīs* and Kṛṣṇa forget that Kṛṣṇa is the Supreme Personality of Godhead and that the *gopīs* are His own pleasure potency. She has arranged that both the *gopīs* and Kṛṣṇa think that the *gopīs* are married to other *gopas*, and therefore they have a paramour relationship with Kṛṣṇa. If it were not like this, there would be no *rasa* at all. *Para* means 'greatest,' one's own greatest wealth (*kīya*), and it also means 'another,' another's wealth. Therefore the meaning in *tattva-siddhānta*, philosophical conclusive truth, and *rasa-tattva* is harmoniously reconciled. Śrīla Rūpa Gosvāmī has explained this, especially in *Ujjvala-nīlamaṇi*, and also in his other books. The *gopīs* are Kṛṣṇa's own power, but for *rasa* it is said that they are *parakīya*.

What is *parakīya*? There are two principles: *ātmā-rasa* and *para-rasa*, or *eka-rasa* and *aneka-rasa*. Kṛṣṇa is *eka-rasa* or *ātmā-rasa*. He is the complete embodiment of *rasa*. He is *ātmārāma* and *āptakāma*, meaning that He is always full and satisfied within Himself, and He doesn't need anything from anyone in order to be happy. The *gopīs* are His power. *Śakti-śaktimatayor abheda*. *Śakti*, the energy, and *śaktimān*, the possessor of that energy, or power, are one. They are identical.

At the same time, although Kṛṣṇa has the quality of being *ātmā-rasa*, He is also *para-rasa*. *Para-rasa* means that the *gopīs* have some specialty that distinguishes them from Kṛṣṇa. Although they are part of Kṛṣṇa, although they are one with Him, their specialty is that they serve Him in the mood of amorous *rasa*. Kṛṣṇa is the enjoyer, and they are the containers or reservoirs of love and affection for Him.

Aneka-rasa or *para-rasa* is the *gopīs' rasa*, or mood of service, which Kṛṣṇa wants to taste in various ways. Their *rasa* is in the form of *parakīya-rasa*, and this is the meaning of *parakīya* – nothing else. These are exalted philosophical truths, which have been also explained by Śrīla Bhaktivinoda Ṭhākura.

> [**Vijaya**: Your statements are astounding. How is it possible that even Kṛṣṇa Himself, who is the embodiment of *rasa* and the constitutional enjoyer of *rasa*, does not fully understand the behavior of *mādana* (the most exalted love for Kṛṣṇa, which is only experienced by Śrīmatī Rādhikā)?
>
> **Gosvāmī**: Kṛṣṇa is *rasa* Himself, and He is unlimited, omniscient, and omnipotent. Nothing is hidden from Him, and nothing is inaccessible or impossible

for Him. He is eternally *eka-rasa*, and at the same time, He is also *aneka-rasa*, due to His *acintya-bhedābheda-dharma* (inconceivable, simultaneous oneness and difference). As *eka-rasa*, encompassing everything within Himself, He is *ātmārāma*, and in this condition, no *rasa* exists separately from Him.

However, He is simultaneously *aneka-rasa*. Thus, besides *ātma-gata-rasa* (*rasa* experienced by oneself), there is also *para-gata-rasa* (*rasa* experienced by others) and the varieties of mixed *ātma-para-vicitra-rasa*. The happiness of His pastimes lies in the latter two types of *rasa*.

When *para-gata* expands to the ultimate degree, it is called *parakīya-rasa*, and this highest development manifests abundantly in Vṛndāvana. Thus, for the *ātma-gata-rasa*, the unknown, exalted, and unique happiness of *parakīya-rasa* is the last limit of *mādana*. This is present during the purely unmanifest pastimes in Goloka, and also to a slight extent in Vraja.][2]

Thus, Jīva Gosvāmī is not of a different opinion than Rūpa Gosvāmī. They have the same opinion. Viśvanātha Cakravartī Ṭhākura has proven that Jīva Gosvāmī was in *parakīya-bhāva*, and that he accepted *Śrīmad-Bhāgavatam* and *Ujjvala-nīlamaṇi*. In his own *Ujjvala-nīlamaṇi ṭīkā*, Śrīla Jīva Gosvāmī has written, "*svecchayā likhitaṁ kiñcit, kiñcid atra parecchayā* – I have written some things by my own desire and some things by the desire of others. The portions which are consistent, in which *svakīya* and *parakīya* are reconciled and in the line of Rūpa Gosvāmī, this is my desire; and the portions that are not reconciled are written due to the desire of others." I have written about all these topics in my book called *Prabandha Pañcakam, Five Essential Essays*. Try to know these truths fully.

2 This insertion is an excerpt from *Jaiva-dharma*, Chapter 36.

Sahajiyā bābājīs say that we Gauḍīya Vaiṣṇavas are not a branch of the line of Madhvācārya. They say that Madhvācārya is of a different opinion than the Gauḍīya Vaiṣṇavas, but this is quite wrong. We have so many specialties that are also present in the line of Madhvācārya.

Also, some of them say that because Caitanya Mahāprabhu took *sannyāsa*, the renounced order, from Keśava Bhāratī, a *māyāvādī*, He Himself must be a *māyāvādī*. We don't accept this. Mahāprabhu's actual *guru* was Īśvara Purīpāda. He took only His *veśa*, saffron cloth, from Keśava Bhāratī, and there is no harm in this. Madhvācārya did this as well.

Sannyāsa can be taken in this way.[3] However, Mahāprabhu took *gopāla-mantra* and other *mantras* from Śrī Īśvara Purīpāda. Mādhavendra Purīpāda also took *sannyāsa* from a *māyāvādī*, but he took *dīkṣā* initiation in the line of Mādhava, and Lakṣmīpati Tīrtha was his *guru*.

We are thus in one line. There is some little difference in *upāsanā-mārga*, worshipping a particular Deity, but by *tattva* we are both the same. Śrī Baladeva Vidyābhūṣaṇa prabhu has written about this very vividly, and the opinion of Kavi-karṇapūra is also that we are in the Madhva *sampradāya*.

Another point is that these *bābājīs* don't accept Śrīla Baladeva Vidyābhūṣaṇa to be in the Gauḍīya Vaiṣṇava line. They are vehemently opposed to this understanding. However, if Baladeva Vidyābhūṣaṇa Prabhu were out of our Gauḍīya *sampradāya*, then who is our savior? He went to Galtā Gaddī in Jaipura and defeated the Vaiṣṇavas of the Śrī *sampradāya*[4], convincing them that Śrīmatī Rādhikā should be established

---

3 See Endnote 1, at the end of this chapter.

4 One of the four authorized Vaiṣṇava *sampradāyas* (lines of disciplic succession), which was originally founded by Śrīmatī Lakṣmī Devī, the goddess of fortune (Śrī is another name of Lakṣmī). In Kali-yuga, Śrī Rāmānuja became the *ācārya* of this *sampradāya* and propounded the Vedānta philosophy of qualified monism (*visistadvaita-vada*).

on the left of Kṛṣṇa (Govinda) in the temple. He wrote a commentary on *Vedānta-sūtra* called *Govinda-bhāṣya*, and that commentary has been accepted as the *Gauḍīya-bhāṣya*, the commentary representing the Gauḍīya *sampradāya*.[5]

If Baladeva Vidyābhūṣaṇa Prabhu is not in our *sampradāya* (the unbroken disciplic line), then what *sampradāya* is he in? All of his commentaries are in the line of Śrīla Rūpa Gosvāmī and our Gauḍīya Vaiṣṇava *ācāryas*. If he were out of our *sampradāya*, everything would have been finished. In other words, if he had not been present at that time in Jaipura, our Gauḍīya Vaiṣṇava identity would have disappeared from this world. This is a vital point.

From Saffron to White to Saffron

These *bābājīs* also say that if anyone wears the saffron cloth of *sannyāsa*, he is not in the Gauḍīya Vaiṣṇava line. They have no correct idea. As stated in *Śrī Caitanya-caritāmṛta* (*Madhya-līlā* 8.128):

kibā vipra, kibā nyāsī, śūdra kene naya
yei kṛṣṇa-tattva-vettā, sei guru haya

[It does not matter whether a person is a *vipra* (learned scholar in Vedic wisdom) or is born in a lower family, or is in the renounced order of life. If he is master in the science of Kṛṣṇa, he is the perfect and bona fide spiritual master.*]

Śrīla Kṛṣṇa dāsa Kavirāja Gosvāmī has written the words *'kibā nyāsī;' nyāsī* means *'sannyāsī.'* Īśvara Purīpāda, Mādhavendra Purīpāda, and all renunciates in their line were *sannyāsīs* in saffron cloth; so many associates of Caitanya Mahāprabhu wore saffron cloth, as did Svarūpa Dāmodara. Saffron cloth is

---

5 See Endnote 2, at the end of this chapter.

the sign of renunciation, and it is also the color of *anurāga*, or attachment, for Kṛṣṇa. It indirectly indicates someone who is not a widow; in other words it indicates someone who is married and has Kṛṣṇa as her beloved. On the other hand, white cloth (in Vedic culture) is worn by widows. We are not widows.

Aware of Śrī Caitanya Mahāprabhu's identity as the Supreme Lord, Śrīla Sanātana Gosvāmī had great honor for His saffron cloth and thought, "I cannot be like Him, I am not so high." Out of reverence he wore a simple white cloth, just to minimize his material necessities, and he used to worship Mahāprabhu's saffron cloth.

In Vraja, the Vrajavāsīs all used to call Sanātana Gosvāmī '*bābā*.' They called him *bara-bābā*, meaning 'elder *sādhu*,' and Rūpa Gosvāmī *choṭa-bābā*, meaning 'younger *sādhu*.' After them, others in their line also took white cloth, but after the time of Viśvanātha Cakravartī Ṭhākura, many persons wearing that cloth deviated.

Some great souls, like Jagannātha dāsa Bābājī, Madhusūdana dāsa Bābājī, and Gaura Kiśora dāsa Bābājī used this *bābājī* title out of humility, and everyone used to call them that. [*bābā* means '*sādhu*' or 'father,' and *jī* is a suffix meaning 'respectable.'] These *mukta-mahā-puruṣas*, great transcendentalists, are *paramahaṁsas*, or swan-like renunciants of the highest spiritual rank, and they are also the eternal associates of Rādhā and Kṛṣṇa. They are far above the conception of *bābājī*, or even *sannyāsa* (which is within the *varṇāśrama* system). For them to accept the title *bābājī*, therefore, is their humility.[6]

At that time, those family persons who were of loose character and had no status in society honored these bogus *bābājīs*.

---

6 Considering that the 'renounced' *bābājī* society was a disgrace to the Vaiṣṇava community, Śrīla Gaura Kiśora dāsa Bābājī Mahārāja once decided to dress up like a sophisticated gentleman so that society members would notice that he was clearly distancing himself from the *bābājī* code of dress and immoral behavior –Ed.

That is why Śrīla Sarasvatī Ṭhākura re-introduced the reddish cloth and *sannyāsa*. And after that he preached throughout the world.

Presently, many persons who were previously in the Gauḍīya Maṭha but due to debauchery were rejected from there, have now become *bābājīs*.

Take Care

If you read these *sahajiyā bābājīs'* books – their translations and commentaries of our *ācārya's* literatures – their poison may enter you.

avaiṣṇava-mukhodgīrṇaṁ pūtaṁ hari-kathāmṛtam
śravaṇaṁ naiva kartavyaṁ sarpocchiṣṭaṁ yathā payaḥ

(*Padma Purāṇa*)

[One should not hear anything about Kṛṣṇa from a non-Vaiṣṇava. Milk touched by the lips of a serpent has poisonous effects. Similarly, talks about Kṛṣṇa given by a non-Vaiṣṇava are also poisonous.*]

Śrīla Raghunātha dāsa Gosvāmī's *Vilāpa-kusumā*ñjali and other books like *Kṛṣṇa-bhāvanāmṛta*, *Rādhā-rāsa-sudhā-nidhi*, and *Stavāvalī* are all good books. They are *amṛta*, nectar. However, if you hear them from non-Vaiṣṇavas, the ideas of such non-Vaiṣṇavas will enter your heart and you will be deviated from the path of *bhaki*. Be very careful about this.

What will become of such speakers and their audiences?

naitat samācarej jātu
manasāpi hy anīśvaraḥ
vinaśyaty ācaran mauḍhyād
yathā 'rudro 'bdhi-jaṁ viṣam

(*Śrīmad-Bhāgavatam* 10.33.31)

[One who is not a great controller should never imitate the behavior of ruling personalities, even mentally. If out of foolishness an ordinary person does imitate such behavior, he will simply destroy himself, just as a person who is not Rudra would destroy himself if he tried to drink an ocean of poison.*]

If someone is not powerful like Śaṅkara (Lord Śiva), yet he wants to drink poison as Śaṅkara did, he will die at once. First be Śaṅkara; first be qualified. Because these *bābājīs* criticize the pure *ācāryas* in the line of Gauḍīya Vaiṣṇavas, we should boycott the books they have translated, even though the books from which these translations are coming are bona fide. If you are qualified like a *haṁsa*, a swan, who can separate milk from water, then you may be protected while reading their translations, otherwise not.

I have come to tell you these things only to make you all careful. Don't be bewildered. Try to be very strong, knowing all these points.

Endnotes

1 An excerpt from Śrīla Bhaktivedānta Svāmī Mahārāja's purport to *Śrī Caitanya-caritāmṛta, Ādi-līlā* 3.34:

During the time of Lord Caitanya, the influence of Śaṅkarācārya in society was very strong. People thought that one could accept *sannyāsa* only in the disciplic succession of Śaṅkarācārya. Lord Caitanya could have performed His missionary activities as a householder, but He found householder life an obstruction to His mission. Therefore He decided to accept the renounced order, *sannyāsa*. Since His acceptance of *sannyāsa* was also designed to attract public attention, Lord Caitanya, not wishing to disturb the social convention, took the renounced order of life from a *sannyāsī* in the disciplic succession of Śaṅkarācārya, although *sannyāsa* was also sanctioned in the Vaiṣṇava *sampradāya*.

2 An excerpt from a lecture by Śrīla Bhaktivedānta Svāmī Mahārāja, spoken on September 30, 1973:

As far as we in the Madhva-Gauḍīya *sampradāya* are concerned, our *ācāryas* accepted *Śrīmad-Bhāgavatam* as the natural commentary on *Brahma-sūtra*. The Gauḍīya *sampradāya* did not make any commentary on the *Brahma-sūtra* because they accepted, and Caitanya Mahāprabhu accepted, *Śrīmad-Bhāgavatam* as the natural commentary because it was also written by Vyāsadeva, the original author of *Brahmā-sūtra*. If the author had made his own commentary, there was no need of another. This is the Gauḍīya Vaiṣṇava *siddhānta*.

Sometime back, however, in Jaipura, there was a challenge that the Gauḍīya *sampradāya* has no commentary on the *Vedānta-sūtra*. Viśvanātha Cakravartī Ṭhākura was requested to go there because he was the most senior Vaiṣṇava scholar. He was living in Vṛndāvana at that time, and because he was very advanced in age at that time, he authorized Baladeva Vidyābhūṣaṇa, "You do it. There is no need, but people are demanding, 'Where is your commentary on the *Vedānta-sūtra*?'" Therefore, by the dictation of Govindajī at Jaipura, Baladeva Vidyābhūṣaṇa wrote the commentary on *Brahma-sūtra* called *Govinda-bhāṣya*. In this way, the Brahmā-Madhva-Gauḍīya *sampradāya* has also got a commentary on *Brahma-sūtra*, and that is required.

Part V

The Sahajiyā Within Us

[In the previous discourses, Śrīla Nārāyaṇa Gosvāmī Mahārāja has educated us regarding the current of unalloyed *bhakti*, and how and why to avoid being derailed by *sahajiyās*. In this discourse and the two discourses in Part VI, he is educating us about how and why to avoid the influence of the *sahajiyā* within our own selves.]

Kṛṣṇa, The Origin of All Existence, The Lord of All Sweetness

The song *Śrī Madhurāṣṭakam* tells us that everything is sweet (*madhura*) about Śrī Kṛṣṇa, the original Lord of sweetness. His Vṛndāvana is sweet, His laughing and smiling are sweet, His coming-and-going is so sweet, His Yamunā and her waves are sweet, His *nikuñjas* (secluded groves wherein He and the *gopīs* perform their confidential amorous pastimes) are sweet, and His sidelong glances are also very sweet.

Who is speaking about the sweetness of Kṛṣṇa here? Is it the evil demons Kaṁsa Mahārāja, Aghāsura, Bakāsura, or Pūtanā? Śrīmatī Rādhikā Herself is uttering this; She alone is fully qualified to speak in this way.

The history behind Rādhikā's words is that a *sakhī* once told Her, "Kṛṣṇa has left Vṛndāvana. He now has 16,108 queens, and numerous others want to marry Him as well. Why do You maintain such great love and affection for that crooked Kṛṣṇa? He has no love for You and no love for Vṛndāvana. Give Him up; try to forget Him forever." Śrīmatī Rādhikā replied, "O *sakhī*, what you are saying is true. But I cannot forget Him, because everything about Him is so sweet."

Demons like Kaṁsa, Jarāsandha, Duryodhana, Keśī, Pūtanā, Bakāsura, Aghāsura, Cāṇūra, and Muṣṭika saw that very same Kṛṣṇa, but they did not see or experience His sweetness at all. Rather, they considered Him a very cruel, powerful, and dangerous enemy.

Sahajiyās Cannot Relish His Sweetness

Do you know why I am speaking in this way? These demons were against Kṛṣṇa, so instead of experiencing His sweetness, they simply experienced their own enmity. Similarly, if we imagine that we are deeply meditating on Kṛṣṇa's *aṣṭa-kālīya-līlā*, His daily twenty-four hour pastimes with the *gopīs*, but we have not reached the stage of *bhāva-bhakti*, we will also not experience His sweetness. Rather, we will experience our own lust and material desires. In this connection, Kaṁsa and other demons represent our material desires.

Kṛṣṇa and the realization of the sweetness of Kṛṣṇa is surely our goal, but do not try to jump up to the top of the tree. Begin from the root of the tree and gradually climb up from there; then you can realize your goal.

The sincere devotee engages in the proper process of *bhakti* from the start. At first he follows the verse beginning with *ādau śraddhā tataḥ sādhu-saṅgo 'tha bhajana-kriyā*[1]. After this, he is able to follow the principles as stated in the verse beginning *kṣāntir avyartha-kālatvaṁ*[2].

The Goal of Bhakti: To Realize and Relish His Sweetness

If you can follow these two *ślokas*, then you can realize something of the goal. I know, and I see, that in Western and Eastern countries many of the devotees try to enter *aṣṭa-kālīya-līlā*, although they know nothing of its transcendental nature. Our Gosvāmīs have warned us not to delve very much into this subject matter.

This topic is truly our goal, and we can realize it by following the proper process. If a person is filled with worldly desires and is attached to women, wine, and wealth, misunderstanding his own identity and considering himself to be his body, how can he properly meditate on *aṣṭa-kālīya-līlā*?

Eroticism Divine and Mundane

Suppose a man or woman try to meditate on Rādhā-Kṛṣṇa's pastimes at midnight. Suppose they try to remember how all the *gopīs* left their homes and met Kṛṣṇa alone, and moreover, how Kṛṣṇa left all the *gopīs* in the middle of the night and took Śrīmatī Rādhikā inside a *kuñja* in which They played together intimately. What will he or she actually think about? Likewise, if such a man and woman meet together at night to discuss these most confidential topics, what will be the ultimate result of their discussion? They are bound to feel lust. They will not be able to control their minds or senses, and their characters and

---

1 Please see page 16 for the full verse and translation.

2 Please see pages 17–18 for the full verse and translation.

entire spiritual lives will be ruined. Do you understand what I am saying? We should not even think about these topics.[3]

A young or even old person may remember the meaning of this verse:

pramada-madana-līlāḥ kandare kandare te
racayati nava-yūnor dvandvam asminn amandam
iti kila kalanārthaṁ lagnakas tad-dvayor me
nija-nikaṭa-nivāsaṁ dehi govardhana! tvam

(*Govardhana-vāsa-prārthanā-daśakam*, Verse 2
by Śrīla Raghunātha dāsa Gosvāmī)

[The youthful Divine Couple perform delightful amorous pastimes within each and every one of your caves. Thus, since you facilitate the witnessing of Their *līlās*, O Govardhana, please give me residence by your side.]

---

3 Śrīla Nārāyaṇa Gosvāmī Mahārāja has personally translated into Hindi some of the Gosvāmīs' literatures that discuss these confidential topics, and he instructed his disciples to translate his works into English and other languages after that. He wanted that there would be authentic translations, publications, and presentations of these esoteric transcendental pastimes – for now and for posterity – so that new- and old-comers would not be inclined to search in the domain of those who are not properly following the teachings of Śrīla Rūpa Gosvāmī and our Gauḍīya *guru-paramparā*.

In May of 2002, while translating *Ujjvala-nīlamaṇi*, he stated, "I am writing about the very elevated moods of Śrīla Rūpa Gosvāmī; moods that were inspired in him by Śrī Caitanya Mahāprabhu Himself. Mahāprabhu ordered him to write about the deep feelings of the *gopīs*, and the process by which we can achieve similar feelings. Most of you are not qualified to hear or read about this, what to speak of follow, and yet we are writing. Otherwise, if we do not do so, these moods will be lost to the world. We must record this for future generations." Later that year, during his Janmāṣṭamī lecture in August, Śrīla Mahārāja told his audience, "If one is qualified he can read *Śrī Ujjvala-nīlamaṇi*, but he must do so under the guidance of exalted Vaiṣṇavas. In this way, by the mercy of *guru*, he can realize all those/these transcendental moods."

He took the responsibility of educating the old- and new-comers how to carefully treat these most confidential, exalted, outstanding literatures, and he desired that his sincere disciples also accept that responsibility –Ed.

This verse suggests that Rādhā and Kṛṣṇa are meeting together and embracing. If a devotee who is not advanced in *bhakti* tries to meditate on this, a worldly conception is bound to come in his heart. Therefore, always be careful.

Śrī Śukadeva Gosvāmī, who is a *mahā-mahā-bhāgavata*, a topmost self-realized soul, is so detached from material consideration and possessions that he does not even possess a *ḍor-kaupīna* (loincloth), nor does he even have a *bhajana kuṭīra*, a place to perform *bhajana*. He is totally renounced. For him there is no difference between the most beautiful naked lady and a piece of dry firewood. He has no interest at all in the affairs of men and women. Yet, that Śukadeva Gosvāmī offers reverential obeisances to *rasa-līlā* and *aṣṭa-kālīya-līlā*. Although service to sweet Kṛṣṇa like that of the *gopīs* is certainly our goal, we cannot pretend to be close to that service at our stage.[4]

Śrīla Viśvanātha Cakravartī Ṭhākura has written:

ārādhyo bhagavān vrajeśa tanayas tad dhāma vṛndāvanaṁ
ramyā kācid upāsanā vrajavadhū vargeṇa yā kalpitā
śrīmad-bhāgavataṁ pramāṇām amalaṁ premā pumārtho mahān
śrī caitanya mahāprabhor matam idaṁ tatrādaro na paraḥ

(*Caitanya-manjusam*)

[Bhagavān Vrajendra-nandana Śrī Kṛṣṇa and His transcendental abode Śrī Vṛndāvana-dhāma are my most worshipable objects. The most excellent method of worshiping Kṛṣṇa is that adopted by the *gopa-ramaṇīs*, the young wives of Vraja. *Śrīmad-Bhāgavatam* is the flawless and most authoritative scripture, and *kṛṣṇa-prema* (pure love for Kṛṣṇa) is the fifth and highest achievement of human life, beyond *dharma* (mundane religion), *artha* (wealth), *kāma* (sense gratification), and *mokṣa* (liberation). This is the opinion of

4 See Endnote 1, at the end of this chapter.

Śrī Caitanya Mahāprabhu. We have supreme regard for this conclusion. We have no inclination or respect for any other cheating opinions.]

The highest examples of love and affection in service to Kṛṣṇa are the *gopīs*. By constitution, conditioned souls of this world do not have the eligibility to become *svatantra nāyakas*, or direct beloveds of Kṛṣṇa, like Śrīmatī Lalitā, Śrīmatī Viśākhā, and others in their category. We conditioned souls have the eligibility to become *mañjarīs*, young maidservants of Śrīmatī Rādhikā, thus serving Kṛṣṇa through Her.

This is not a small attainment. This most exalted service is so confidential that it cannot be performed by even Lalitā or Viśākhā, or by others like them, even though these *svatantra nāyakas* are on a higher rank than the *mañjarīs*. Such service can only be executed by *gopīs* like Śrī Rūpa Mañjarī and Śrī Rati Mañjarī. Lalitā and Viśākhā cannot enter a *kuñja* in which Rādhā and Kṛṣṇa are alone and engaged in Their most intimate amorous pastimes, but the *mañjarīs* can enter without hesitation and serve both Rādhā and Kṛṣṇa there.

An Obstacle on the Path of Bhakti

Do not discuss the confidential matters of Śrī Śrī Rādhā-Kṛṣṇa before the general public or any neophyte audience. Be careful, otherwise your audiences of the opposite gender will be charmed by hearing from you; they will weep and run after you, and your character will be lost forever.

The Clear Path

Always try to follow the teachings of the Eleventh Canto of *Śrīmad-Bhāgavatam*, and try to follow Śrīla Rūpa Gosvāmī's *Upadeśāmṛta* and Śrīla Raghunātha dāsa Gosvāmī's *Śrī Manaḥ-śikṣā*. This is first. Then try to gradually come to the stage of *rati* (*bhāva-bhakti*), at which time all of Kṛṣṇa's pastimes will automatically manifest in a very pure form. Try to follow these instructions. Go through the channel opened by Śrīla Bhaktivinoda Ṭhākura and by our *guru-paramparā*, and especially by Śrīla Rūpa Gosvāmī and Śrīla Raghunātha dāsa Gosvāmī.

In *Śrīmad-Bhāgavatam*, Śrī Kṛṣṇa-dvaipāyana Vyāsa and Śrīla Śukadeva Gosvāmī have somewhat explained about the goal of our life in the descriptions of Kṛṣṇa's incarnations like Matsya, Kūrma, Varāha, Nṛsiṁha, Rāma, Paraśurāma, Vāmana, and Kalki. They have kept all the *madhura-līlā*, the descriptions of Kṛṣṇa and His associates in Vṛndāvana, and especially the descriptions of the *gopīs*, in the Tenth Canto, and there they explained our aim and object fully.

Kṛṣṇa Himself manifested as each of the incarnations. They are all the same Kṛṣṇa, but He is playing the role of being Them.

Śrī Jayadeva Gosvāmī sings in his *Śrī Daśāvatāra-stotram* (Verse 11):

> *śrī-jayadeva-kaver idam uditam udāraṁ*
> *śṛṇu sukha-daṁ śubha-daṁ bhava-sāram*
> *keśava! dhṛta-daśa-vidha-rūpa! jaya jagadīśa! hare*

> [Please hear this sincere prayer uttered by the poet Śrī Jayadeva. It awards happiness and auspiciousness and describes the essence of Your incarnations. O Keśava, who assumed ten forms! All glories to You, O Lord of the Universe, O Hari!]

In this connection, Keśava refers to Vrajendra-nandana Śrī Kṛṣṇa. That same Kṛṣṇa is our goal, and to serve Him as the *gopīs* do is certainly our goal. At the same time, without being very careful, you will be following the path of the great demons Pūtanā, Aghāsura, Bakāsura, and Kaṁsa. You will be bound to be like them.

Śrīla Śukadeva Gosvāmī began speaking about the topics of *bhakti* from its beginning stages, as well as the processes to achieve the various stages of *bhakti*. Then, in the Eleventh Canto he discussed the process Śrī Nārada Muni explained to Vāsudeva about the topics instructed by the Nava-yogendras to Mahārāja Nimi. For example, the Nava-yogendras explained about the twenty-four *gurus*, including the air and the Earth (planet). From the air one can learn detachment, and from the Earth one can learn tolerance. In those texts the processes to achieve the highest goal given in the Tenth Canto has also been explained.

The same goal of life has been expressed in a still better way in *Śrī Caitanya-caritāmṛta*. In the very beginning of that *śāstra*, Śrīla Kṛṣṇadāsa Kavirāja Gosvāmī has shared Śrīla Rūpa Gosvāmī's words:

anarpita-carīṁ cirāt karuṇayāvatīrṇaḥ kalau
samarpayitum unnatojjvala-rasāṁ sva-bhakti-śriyam
hariḥ puraṭa-sundara-dyuti-kadamba-sandīpitaḥ
sadā hṛdaya-kandare sphuratu vaḥ śacī-nandanaḥ

(*Śrī Caitanya-caritāmṛta, Ādi-līlā* 1.4)

[May the Supreme Lord who is known as the son of Śrīmatī Śacī-devī (Śacīnandana), be transcendentally situated in the innermost chambers of your heart. Resplendent with the radiance of molten gold, He has appeared in the Age of Kali by His causeless mercy to bestow what no incarnation has ever offered before: the most sublime and radiant mellow of devotional service, the mellow of conjugal love.*]

śrī-rādhāyāḥ praṇaya-mahimā kīdṛśo vānayaivā-
svādyo yenādbhuta-madhurimā kīdṛśo vā madīyaḥ
saukhyaṁ cāsyā mad-anubhavataḥ kīdṛśaṁ veti lobhāt
tad-bhāvāḍhyaḥ samajani śacī-garbha-sindhau harīnduḥ

(*Śrī Caitanya-caritāmṛta, Ādi-līlā* 1.6)

> [Desiring to understand the glory of Rādhārāṇī's love, the wonderful qualities in Him that She alone relishes through Her love, and the happiness She feels when She realizes the sweetness of His love, the Supreme Lord Hari, richly endowed with Her emotions, appeared from the womb of Śrīmatī Śacī-devī, as the moon appeared from the ocean.*]

rādhā kṛṣṇa-praṇaya-vikṛtir hlādinī śaktir asmād
ekātmānāv api bhuvi purā deha-bhedaṁ gatau tau
caitanyākhyaṁ prakaṭam adhunā tad-dvayaṁ caikyam āptaṁ
rādhā-bhāva-dyuti-suvalitaṁ naumi kṛṣṇa-svarūpam

(*Śrī Caitanya-caritāmṛta, Ādi-līlā* 1.5)

> [The loving affairs of Śrī Rādhā and Kṛṣṇa are transcendental manifestations of the Lord's internal pleasure-giving potency. Although Rādhā and Kṛṣṇa are one in Their identity, They separated Themselves eternally. Now these two transcendental identities have again united, in the form of Śrī Kṛṣṇa Caitanya. I bow down to Him, who has manifested Himself with the sentiment and complexion of Śrīmatī Rādhārāṇī although He is Kṛṣṇa Himself.*]

Śrīla Kṛṣṇadāsa Kavirāja Gosvāmī especially explained the goal and the process to achieve it in the fourth chapter of *Śrī Caitanya-caritāmṛta, Ādi-līlā*, and in *Śrī Rāya Rāmānanda Saṁvāda*. Śrī Caitanya Mahāprabhu also instructed the process to Śrīla Rūpa Gosvāmī in *Madhya-līlā*, chapters nineteen and twenty, and to Śrīla Sanātana Gosvāmī in *Madhya-līlā*, chapters twenty to twenty-three. Let us take care about trying to jump to the top of a tree while being at the bottom. If you enter a fire, you will be burned.

At the same time, it is also not sufficient to merely speak about the philosophical truths and processes of *bhakti*. Try to be actually established, or realized, in this. Suppose a disciple is always preaching the glories of Kṛṣṇa's philosophy and His variety of sweet pastimes. Suppose that disciple is always chanting. He is chanting one *lākha* (sixty-four rounds) of holy names daily and is always reading about the pastimes of Kṛṣṇa and glorifying Him – but he does not have very much faith in his *guru* and he does not follow his *gurudeva's* orders. Or, he sometimes follows and sometimes does not; sometimes he follows his uncontrolled mind.

It is stated in the *Upaniṣads*:

yasya deve parā bhaktir
yathā deve tathā gurau
tasyaite kathitā hy arthāh
prakāśante mahātmānaḥ

(*Śvetāśvatara Upaniṣad* 6.23)

[Only unto those great souls who have implicit faith in both the Lord and the spiritual master are all the imports of Vedic knowledge automatically revealed.*]

Endnote

1 An excerpt from Śrīla Bhaktivedānta Svāmī Mahārāja's purport to *Śrīmad-Bhāgavatam* 1.4.5:

In the *Bhagavad-gītā* (5.18) it is said that a learned sage looks equally on a learned and gentle *brāhmaṇa* (priest or teacher of divine knowledge), a *caṇḍāla* (dog-eater), a dog or a cow due to his spiritual vision. Śrīla Śukadeva Gosvāmī attained that stage. Thus he did not see a male or female; he saw all living entities in different dress. The ladies who were bathing could understand the mind of a man simply by studying his demeanor, just as by looking at a child one can understand how innocent he is.

Śukadeva Gosvāmī was a young boy sixteen years old, and therefore all the parts of his body were developed. He was naked also, and so were the ladies. But because Śukadeva Gosvāmī was transcendental to sex relations, he appeared very innocent. The ladies, by their special qualifications, could sense this at once, and therefore they were not very concerned about him. But when his father passed, the ladies quickly dressed. The ladies were exactly like his children or grandchildren, yet they reacted to the presence of Vyāsadeva according to the social custom because Śrīla Vyāsadeva played the part of a householder. A householder has to distinguish between a male and female, otherwise he cannot be a householder.

One should, therefore, attempt to know the distinction between body and soul without any attachment for male and female. As long as such distinction is there, one should not try to become a *sannyāsī* like Śukadeva Gosvāmī.

Part VI

This Is The Question

Why Not Only One Book?

I have come here to share with you the teachings of Śrī Caitanya Mahāprabhu.

śrī-caitanya-mano-'bhīṣṭaṁ sthāpitaṁ yena bhūtale
svayaṁ rūpaḥ kadā mahyaṁ dadāti sva-padāntikam

(*Śrī Prema-bhakti-candrikā*,
by Śrīla Narottama dāsa Ṭhākura)

Śrī Rūpa Gosvāmī knew the mood of Śrī Caitanya Mahāprabhu, because Mahāprabhu had inspired in his heart the contents of His own heart regarding the reason He descended from Goloka-Vṛndāvana to this world. It was in Prayāga that the Lord first inspired in his heart His own aim and objective. Then in Purī He requested Śrī Nityānanda Prabhu, Śrī Svarūpa Dāmodara, Śrī Rāya Rāmānanda, and all His personal associates to bestow their mercy upon Śrīla Rūpa Gosvāmī, so that Rūpa Gosvāmī could establish in this world His innermost desire. By Mahāprabhu's inspiration and mercy, Rūpa Gosvāmī was then able to write *Bhakti-rasāmṛta-sindhu, Ujjvala-nīlamaṇi, Lalita-mādhava, Vidagdha-mādhava*, and so many other books.

Śrī Caitanya Mahāprabhu is not only Caitanya Mahāprabhu. He is Śrī Kṛṣṇa Himself, having taken the beauty and internal moods of Śrīmatī Rādhikā. Whatever He could not give in Kṛṣṇa's pastimes, He gave as Mahāprabhu – as Śacīnandana Gaurahari[1].

Kṛṣṇa had four reasons for descending from Goloka-Śvetadvīpa[2] to this world.

anarpita-carīṁ cirāt karuṇayāvatīrṇaḥ kalau
samarpayitum unnatojjvala-rasāṁ sva-bhakti-śriyam
hariḥ puraṭa-sundara-dyuti-kadamba-sandīpitaḥ
sadā hṛdaya-kandare sphuratu vaḥ śacī-nandanaḥ

(*Śrī Caitanya-caritāmṛta, Ādi-līlā* 1.4)

[May the Supreme Lord who is known as the son of Śrīmatī Śacī-devī (Śacīnandana), be transcendentally situated in the innermost chambers of your heart. Resplendent with the radiance of molten gold, He has appeared in the Age of Kali by His causeless mercy to bestow what no incarnation has ever offered before: the most sublime and radiant mellow of devotional service, the mellow of conjugal love.*]

Kṛṣṇa's primary internal reason was that He wanted to relish the internal moods of Śrīmatī Rādhikā. He considered that although He is so beautiful and sweet, He could not experience what it is in Him that makes Her so maddened.

śrī-rādhāyāḥ praṇaya-mahimā kīdṛśo vānayaivā-
svādyo yenādbhuta-madhurimā kīdṛśo vā madīyaḥ

---

1 When Mahāprabhu was in the *āśrama* of a householder, he was known by the name of Śacīnandana Gaurahari, or 'the son of Śacī, who took the inner moods and golden complexion of Śrīmatī Rādhikā.'

2 Goloka-Śvetadvīpa is that quadrangular section of Goloka-Vṛndāvana where Śrī Caitanya Mahāprabhu and His associates eternally reside. Also see Endnote 1.

saukhyaṁ cāsyā mad-anubhavataḥ kīdṛśaṁ veti lobhāt
tad-bhāvāḍhyaḥ samajani śacī-garbha-sindhau harīnduḥ
(*Śrī Caitanya-caritāmṛta, Ādi-līlā* 1.6)

He could not relish Himself to the extent She could. Thus, He wanted to know the glory of Her love, the nature of the qualities within Him that madden Her so, and the pleasure She experiences by remembering Him. The mood He thus relished is called *unnatojjvala-parakīya-bhāva* (also known as *aupapatya bhāva*), the most brilliant mood of a transcendental paramour.

He wanted to give His mercy: *karuṇayāvatīrṇaḥ kalau samarpayitum unnatojjvala-rasāṁ sva-bhakti-śriyam. Sva-bhakti-śriyam* refers to *mañjarī-bhāva*, the mood of Śrīmatī Rādhikā's maidservant. Since Mahāprabhu especially desired to give this one gift, and He did so, why did Śrīla Rūpa Gosvāmī write so many books, including *Bhakti-rasāmṛta-sindhu* and *Upadeśāmṛta*? Why did he not write only about the topics of *mañjarī-bhāva*, exclaiming, "Oh, all of you devotees throughout the world should accept only *mañjarī-bhāva*"? Why did he not write only one book, saying, "You are all *mañjarīs*"? Why? This is the question.

Are all devotees in only one stage of *bhakti*, or are they in different stages? Actually, there are millions of stages of *bhakti*, and one *mañjarī-bhāva*. *Mañjarī-bhāva* is certainly our highest aim and object, but Śrīla Rūpa Gosvāmī has written in his *Bhakti-rasāmṛta-sindhu*:

śravaṇotkīrtanādīni-vaidha bhakty uditāni tu
yānyaṅgāni ca tānyatra vijñeyāni manīṣibhiḥ
(*Bhakti-rasāmṛta-sindhu* 1.2.296)

[Those who are well-versed in transcendental knowledge (*tattva-vit*) know full well that all the various limbs of *bhakti*, such as *śravaṇa* and loud *kīrtana*, should also be practiced in *rāgānuga-bhakti*.]

He has also written:

sevā sādhaka-rūpeṇa siddha-rupeṇa cātra hi
tad bhāva lipsunā kāryā vraja lokānusārataḥ

(*Bhakti-rasāmṛta-sindhu* 1.2.295)

One will have to follow the *rūpānuga* Vaiṣṇavas, in their *sādhaka-rūpeṇa*, their forms as devotional practitioners, and in their *siddha-rūpeṇa*, their fully perfect forms as associates of Śrī Śrī Rādhā and Kṛṣṇa. We should follow *sādhaka-rūpeṇa* in the teachings of Śrīla Rūpa Gosvāmī regarding the limbs of *bhakti*, the rules and regulations. On one hand, *rūpānuga-bhakti* does not manifest simply by reading *śāstra* or by following rules and regulations, but you must know that in order to have greed for *rūpānuga-bhakti*, it is essential to observe the *śāstric* injunctions. You will have to obey *śāstra*, otherwise you will simply create disturbance in *bhakti*.

śruti-smṛti-purāṇādi-pañcarātra-vidhiṁ vinā
aikāntikī harer bhaktir utpātāyaiva kalpate

(*Bhakti-rasāmṛta-sindhu* 1.2.101)

[Devotional service of the Lord that ignores the authorized Vedic literatures like the Upaniṣads, Purāṇas and *Nārada-pañcarātra* is simply an unnecessary disturbance in society.*]

The meaning of *sevā sādhaka-rūpeṇa siddha-rūpeṇa cātra hi* is that the *rāgānuga-bhakta*, or more specifically, the *rūpānuga-bhakta* will follow the rules and regulations of *bhakti* as Śrīla Raghunātha dāsa Gosvāmī did externally, and internally he will follow the mood of Rati Mañjarī (Śrīla Raghunātha dāsa Gosvāmī's form in Rādhā-Kṛṣṇa's pastimes). Those who have no greed, that is, those who are not at the stage of *bhāva-bhakti*, will not be able to follow him.

It is necessary to follow all the instructions written in *Upadeśāmṛta*. If you boycott *Upadeśāmṛta*, your *bhakti* will be only illusory; it will cheat you. Try to follow Śrīla Rūpa Gosvāmī, who is *akhaṇḍa-guru-tattva*, the complete undivided principle of *guru*.

Not everyone is in the same stage of *bhakti*. Everyone is in different stages. If one is a neophyte and does not have even *śraddhā* (faith in the words of Kṛṣṇa, *guru*, and Vaiṣṇavas), how can you tell him, "You are a *mañjarī*; book your ticket for only the *mañjarī* mood"? I want to tell you all, that this is a very wrong idea. Try to truly understand and then follow the real meaning of *rūpānuga*.

When Nityānanda Prabhu preached in the assembly of Jagāī and Madhāī, they beat Him and blood flowed from His head, but still He gave them *kṛṣṇa-prema*. He preached throughout Bengal and other parts of India, but what was He preaching? Did He preach, "Oh, you are a *mañjarī*"? He never did so.

Nityānanda Prabhu is the root *akhaṇḍa-guru-tattva*. Does He have the mood of a *mañjarī* or not? Yes, he is Anaṅga Mañjarī, but he did not preach about this. One may think, "He does not have a *mañjarī* mood and He did not preach it, so He is not *guru*. I will not obey Him. I will obey only Śrīla Rūpa Gosvāmī." A person who thinks in this way is bogus. He is an offender at the lotus feet of the entire *guru-paramparā*.

We will have to obey the entire *guru-paramparā*. My disciples who are preaching Kṛṣṇa's holy name know what is the mood of the *mañjarīs*, but not all of them are qualified to have it. Be very careful about this. Don't commit offenses at the lotus feet of Vaiṣṇavas. Suppose someone says, "If there is a difference of opinion between Gurudeva and Araṇya Mahārāja [later to become Prema-prayojana dāsa], I will follow Araṇya Mahārāja and not Gurudeva." What is this? This is called *guror-avajñā* (neglecting the authority of *gurudeva* and disobeying his instructions). It is only because of Gurudeva that Araṇya Mahārāja, or any other disciple, knows who is Śrīla Rūpa Gosvāmī and what is the mood of a *mañjarī*. This is a bogus idea. If you have this idea, then kindly correct your feelings; otherwise all your 'moods' will vanish. I have told this to all of you, because nowadays a wind is blowing in this direction: "We will follow only the mood of the *mañjarīs*; nothing else, nothing else, and nothing else."

Only if a real transcendental greed has entered your heart to serve Śrī Rādhā and Kṛṣṇa do these symptoms manifest:

> ["When *bhāva-bhakti*, the seed of ecstatic emotion for Kṛṣṇa, fructifies, the following nine symptoms manifest in one's behavior: forgiveness, concern that time should not be wasted, detachment, absence of false prestige, hope, eagerness, a taste for chanting the holy name of the Lord, attachment to hear the descriptions of the transcendental qualities of the Lord, and affection for those places where the Lord resides – a temple or a holy place like Vṛndāvana. These are all called *anubhāvas*, subordinate signs of ecstatic emotion. They are visible in a person in whose heart the seed of love of God has begun to fructify"* (*Bhakti-rasāmṛta-sindhu* 1.3.25–26).]

Śrīmad-Bhāgavatam is the spotless evidence regarding Śrī Kṛṣṇa's transcendental pastimes and any other transcendental topic. But is the *mañjarī* mood directly written about anywhere in *Śrīmad-Bhāgavatam*? It is not, although it is indirectly indicated in many places. There is even no direct mention of the name 'Śrīmatī Rādhikā,' 'Lalitā,' or 'Viśākhā.' Why is this so? Did Śrīla Vyāsadeva or Śrīla Śukadeva Gosvāmī not know their names? On the contrary, Śrīla Śukadeva Gosvāmī would faint when uttering Rādhikā's name.

Since *Śrīmad-Bhāgavatam* has not openly declared the *mañjarī* mood, we also should not do so. We are not greater than Śrī Vyāsadeva, Śrīla Śukadeva Gosvāmī, Śrīla Rūpa Gosvāmī or Śrī Caitanya Mahāprabhu. We should keep that mood in our hearts, as a wife who has a paramour does not give her husband any such indication. In India it is done like this, but not in the West. Westerners can declare more than ten husbands at a time, but in India, to declare another beloved would create a very big problem.

I request that if you think you have greed for the mood of a *mañjarī*, keep it in your heart so that nobody can have a scent of it. Otherwise, in a day or two you may commit offenses and your mood will disappear forever. This is not a subject for preaching everywhere in the marketplace. Keep it inside, like camphor. If camphor burns at an open doorway it evaporates, whereas if it is kept hidden behind closed doors, its fragrance will increase. It is very good if one has actual greed. I appreciate this, and I offer my heartfelt blessings to you if you have this. But keep it in your heart and don't disturb others, otherwise they will end up collecting so many lady friends and engage in so-called *parakīya* mood, meaning illicit and immoral connection with the opposite sex.

My request is this: do not be mad to be a *mañjarī*. First try to follow *Śrī Upadeśāmṛta*, and then the other writings of Śrīla Rūpa Gosvāmī. You can then gradually reach the top of the *bhakti* tree. Don't try to jump at once to the top of the tree, otherwise you may fall down, break your arms and legs, and crack your head. So be careful.

No Part to Disregard

Śrīmad-Bhāgavatam is the pure evidence regarding transcendental subjects. The writer, or manifester, of *Śrīmad-Bhāgavatam* is *mahā-muni* Śrīla Vyāsadeva, who is Śrī Kṛṣṇa

Himself, and therefore there can be nothing wrong in it. Śrīla Vyāsadeva has written this in the first chapter of the first canto, and Śrīla Śukadeva Gosvāmī has repeated it:

nigama-kalpa-taror galitaṁ phalaṁ
śuka-mukhād amṛta-drava-saṁyutam
pibata bhāgavataṁ rasam ālayam
muhur aho rasikā bhuvi bhāvukāḥ

(*Śrīmad-Bhāgavatam* 1.1.3)

Śrīmad-Bhāgavatam is Kṛṣṇa Himself, and it is the essence of the entire Vedic literature – Veda, Vedānta, the Upaniṣads, the Purāṇas, and so on. Being the essence of all Vedic scriptures, there is nothing in it to be disregarded. It is a nectarean fruit coming through the *guru-paramparā* from transcendental Vṛndāvana.

Śrīla Śukadeva Gosvāmī is also in the *guru-paramparā*, and he has brought the fruit that is without any skin or seed. Thus, there is no part of it to discard. It is very amazing – it is coming all the way from the spiritual world to this planet, containing nothing but sweet juice, and yet it has not broken.

We should hear *Śrīmad-Bhāgavatam* from the first canto to the last, the twelfth canto, as each and every canto is the essence of the entire Vedic literature. Śrīla Vyāsadeva has requested us to drink this entire nectar-fruit of *Śrīmad-Bhāgavatam* through our ears – not our mouth, but our ears. If one thinks that we should only hear the tenth canto, namely the chapters called *Rāsa-līlā*, *Gopī-gīta*, *Yugala-gīta*, and *Bhramara-gīta*, that person is disobeying Śrīla Vyāsadeva. That person's idea is wrong and offensive.

One may say, "Why should we hear about Dhruva Mahārāja? He does not have the mood of a *gopī*. Why should we hear about Prahlāda Mahārāja? Why should we hear about Lord

Nṛsiṁhadeva, Kalki, Vāmana, Varāha, and the rest of the ten incarnations? And why should we hear about Citraketu Mahārāja and Ambarīṣa Mahārāja? We should only search out *Gopī-gīta*."

This idea is wrong. We must hear the entire *Śrīmad-Bhāgavatam*, because Śrī Kṛṣṇa is Nṛsiṁha, Kṛṣṇa is Vāmana, Kṛṣṇa is Rāma, and He is all the other incarnations. Kṛṣṇa wants to hear the glories of all the devotees who have *mamatā*, a sense of 'mine-ness' towards Him. All the devotees who worship Nṛsiṁha, Kalki, Vāmana, Rāma, and Lakṣmī-Nārāyaṇa are actually devotees of Kṛṣṇa, because there is no one other than Kṛṣṇa, the *advaya-jñāna-paratattva*, the one-without-a-second Supreme Absolute Truth. In this way, no part of *Śrīmad-Bhāgavatam* may be neglected.

For example, Hanumān is a *premī-bhakta*, and he has a great sense of mine-ness, or possessiveness, towards Lord Rāma. But who is Rāma? Rāma is Kṛṣṇa Himself. Kṛṣṇa has manifested Himself in that form in order to establish *maryāda*, or ideal behavior. The devotees of all Kṛṣṇa's manifestations are devotees of Kṛṣṇa, so why should we neglect them?

Once, in Naimiṣāraṇya, 88,000 learned and realized scholars gathered to hear from Śrī Sūta Gosvāmī, the disciple of Śrīla Śukadeva Gosvāmī. Śrī Sūta Gosvāmī was a most learned scholar of all Vedic literature and a fully self-realized soul. His *guru*, by whose mercy he was empowered, was *akhaṇḍa-guru-tattva* Śrī Baladeva Prabhu.

The sages told Śrī Sūta Gosvāmī that Kali-yuga, the Iron Age, has now arrived. In this Age lives are short. It is very rare that in this world one will live to be one hundred years of age. Two, three, four, or ten may live that long, but not more than that. Some die in their mother's womb, and some die by accident. They may die at the age of ten, twenty, thirty, fifty, or sixty.

And they are not intelligent. They may say, "We scientists and doctors know more than God." In reality, however, all those who do not perform *bhajana* of Kṛṣṇa are foolish – top to bottom. *Śrīmad-Bhāgavatam* has stated that those who do not engage in *bhajana* of Kṛṣṇa, especially those who do not engage in *uttama-bhakti*, pure, unalloyed devotional service, are foolish like donkeys. They know only sense gratification, and they are very lusty and angry.

They work in order to enjoy happiness, but they get only problems. Their life is full of problems everywhere – problems between husband and wife, son and father, mother and son, neighbors, and everyone else. There are always differences of opinions that they are not able to reconcile.

The sages, headed by Śaunaka Ṛṣi, continued, "You are a learned scholar in all the Vedic truths. We request you to please tell us how our souls can be happy. We are not asking how these bodies can be happy. We know that we are not this physical body, which is only a bag of blood, urine, and other contaminated things."

Śrīla Sūta Gosvāmī said, "I am very happy. By your questions, you have reminded me about the sweet pastimes of Kṛṣṇa." He then replied to the sages' questions regarding the means of happiness:

sa vai puṁsāṁ paro dharmo
yato bhaktir adhokṣaje
ahaituky apratihatā
yayātmā suprasīdati

(*Śrīmad-Bhāgavatam* 1.2.6)

There are two meanings to the phrase *yayātmā suprasīdati* in this verse. One is that if Kṛṣṇa is pleased with us, we are pleased. No pure devotee wants his own happiness; he wants only to make Kṛṣṇa happy. If Kṛṣṇa is served, he will be happy.

The second meaning is that the Supreme Soul is happy by our hearing about Him, and we will be happy by hearing His sweet pastimes.

Regarding the phrase *paro dharmo*, the meaning is that the *dharma*, or religion, of all living beings is certainly, definitely, and only that which is truly *parama-dharma*. There are a variety of religious beliefs, like Islam, Hinduism, Christianity, Buddhism, and so on, but these are not really pure religions or *parama-dharma*, for they are followed only to peacefully maintain our body.

Parama-dharma is the religion of our transcendental soul, and it may reach up to the moods of the *gopīs*. The Vrajavāsīs have that sense of mine-ness, and with that they serve Kṛṣṇa in so many ways – in *śānta* (neutral), *dāsya* (servitorship), *sakhya* (friendship), *vātsalya* (parenthood), and *mādhurya* (conjugal) relationships. Citraketu Mahārāja, Prahlāda Mahārāja are also engaged in *parama-dharma*. In Goloka Vṛndāvana, Kṛṣṇa's servants like Citraka and Patraka are engaged in *parama-dharma*, as are His friends like Subala, Śrīdāmā, and Madhumaṅgala. Mother Yaśodā and Nanda Bābā are also engaged in *parama-dharma*, but it especially refers to the service of the *gopīs*. And among them, Śrīmatī Rādhikā's service is especially *parama-dharma*. But this stage of *parama-dharma* is very rare; the followers of the *gopīs'* moods are very rare. It has been told in *Śrīmad-Bhāgavatam*:

naṣṭa-prāyeṣv abhadreṣu
nityaṁ bhāgavata-sevayā
bhagavaty uttama-śloke
bhaktir bhavati naiṣṭhikī

(*Śrīmad-Bhāgavatam* 1.2.18)

If a devotee is free from most *anarthas* (unwanted habits and mentalities), with only some trace remaining, and that devotee continuously serves *bhakta-bhāgavata* (the pure devotee) and *grantha-bhāgavata* (the Vedic scriptures), his *bhakti* very soon reaches the stage of *niṣṭhā*, or steadiness in *bhakti*. Even this class of persons is very rare, so you can imagine how far away the *gopīs'* mood is and how rare are the followers of the *gopīs'* moods in this world.

So, *parama-dharma* ultimately means 'supreme religion,' the transcendental religion of Vraja. It is the *bhakti* of the Vrajavāsīs, and especially the *bhakti* within the heart of Śrīmatī Rādhikā. We cannot follow Śrīmatī Rādhikā's *bhakti*, but we can follow the *bhakti* of Her maidservants.

You are extremely lucky to be in the line of Śrī Caitanya Mahāprabhu and Śrīla Rūpa Gosvāmī. You have heard their teachings from Vaiṣṇavas, especially from *vraja-rasika* Vaiṣṇavas, and you have read some books also. But please examine your heart to see whether or not you have reached the stage of *niṣṭhā*. If some worldly desires are present in your heart, you have not attained even *niṣṭhā*.

Kṛṣṇa is *adhokṣaja*, beyond our intelligence. The organs of our body are material and thus cannot touch Him; they cannot touch even His *hari-kathā*, His glorification. One's *bhakti* must be *ahaitukī*, causeless. It must be unconditional and without any interruption, flowing forth without interruption, as honey flows from a jar. Then only will one's soul be happy.

By the mercy of Śrī Caitanya Mahāprabhu, Śrīla Rūpa Gosvāmī knew His heart, and he has thus given the definition of *bhakti* in a new way, including all the previous definitions:

anyābhilāṣitā-sūnyaṁ
jñāna-karmādy-anāvṛtam
ānukūlyena kṛṣṇānu-
śilanaṁ bhaktir uttamā

(*Bhakti-rasāmṛta-sindhu* 1.1.11)

[*Uttama-bhakti* is the cultivation of activities that are meant exclusively for the pleasure of Śrī Kṛṣṇa. It is the uninterrupted flow of service to Him, performed through all endeavors of the body, mind, and speech, and through the expression of various spiritual sentiments (*bhāvas*). It is not covered by *jñāna* (knowledge aimed at impersonal liberation) and *karma* (reward-seeking activity), *yoga* or austerities, and it is completely free from all desires other than the aspiration to bring happiness to Kṛṣṇa.]

And, in this connection, it is stated in the beginning of *Śrīmad-Bhāgavatam*:

dharmaḥ projjhita-kaitavo 'tra paramo nirmatsarāṇāṁ satāṁ
vedyaṁ vāstavam atra vastu śivadaṁ tāpa-trayonmūlanam
śrīmad-bhāgavate mahā-muni-kṛte kiṁ vā parair īśvaraḥ
sadyo hṛdy avarudhyate 'tra kṛtibhiḥ śuśrūṣubhis tat-kṣaṇāt
(*Śrīmad-Bhāgavatam* 1.1.2)

[Completely rejecting all religious activities which are materially motivated, this *Bhāgavata Purāṇa* propounds the highest truth, which is understandable by those devotees who are fully pure in heart. The highest truth is reality distinguished from illusion for the welfare of all. Such truth uproots the threefold miseries. This beautiful *Bhāgavatam*, compiled by the great sage Vyāsadeva in his maturity, is sufficient in itself for God realization. What is the need of any other scripture? As soon as one attentively and submissively hears the message of *Bhāgavatam*, by this culture of knowledge the Supreme Lord is established within his heart.*]

Śrīla Viśvanātha Cakravartī Ṭhākura has given a complete explanation of this verse in his *Bhakti-rasāmṛta-sindhu-bindu*.

If we understand and follow Śrīla Rūpa Gosvāmī's definition and Śrīla Viśvanātha Cakravartī Ṭhākura's explanation, if we engage in causeless and continuous *bhakti* under the guidance of *guru* and *rasika* Vaiṣṇavas, then very soon, in a couple of days or maybe at once, all kinds of knowledge and realization of all topics up to *sneha, māna, praṇaya, rāga, anurāga, bhāva, mahābhāva, aniruddha, mohana,* and *mādana* will manifest in us. In addition, at that time renunciation will also come. This is the process of *bhakti*. If you will hear *Bhāgavatam*, or even if you are not hearing but you desire to hear, Kṛṣṇa will know this. *Bhakti* will come, and Kṛṣṇa will be controlled and captured in your heart.

I am finishing here. Please think over the contents of this class during the night. Don't sleep. Think about what we have given today, the explanation of pure, *uttama-bhakti*. I know that it is very rare if one can follow this. Yet, if you practice again and again, again and again, continuously, this *vraja-bhakti* will come.

Endnote

1 An excerpt from Śrīla Bhaktivinoda Ṭhākura's purport on Śrī *Brahmā-saṁhitā* 5.5:

Śrī Jīva Gosvāmī has stated in *Śrī Gopāla-campū*: "That supreme planet is called Goloka because it is the residence of the cows (*go*) and the cowherds (*gopa*). This is the prominent location of the *rāsa-līlā*, which is Śrī Kṛṣṇa's very self. That topmost realm is also known as Śvetadvīpa in the form of the primary place for relishing the *rasa* of several varieties of spiritual sentiments, which are of exactly the same sort of inconceivable nature. It is an exceptionally pure manifestation, for it is untouched by associates possessed of other types of *bhāva*. Thus, these two *svarūpas* of Parama-Goloka and Parama-Śvetadvīpa exist in the undivided form of Goloka-dhāma."

The fundamental purport of this statement is that even after tasting His own pastimes in the form of *vraja-līlā*, Kṛṣṇa had not attained the happiness derived from relishing *rasa* completely. Therefore, Vrajendra-nandana Śrī Kṛṣṇa accepted the internal mood and golden luster of Śrī Rādhikā, who is the supermost abode of *kṛṣṇa-rasa*. The compartment (*prakoṣṭha*) of Goloka where He eternally manifests the pastime of completely tasting *rasa* to the superlative degree is called Śvetadvīpa.

Part VII

Pure Bhakti

Mahāprabhu's Pure Process

Śrī Caitanya Mahāprabhu has explained that *gopī-bhāva* is *dharma* that is related to the *ātmā* (the natural propensity of the soul), but the *prākṛta-sahajiyās* think that it is the *dharma* of the body.

antare niṣṭhā kara, bāhye loka-vyavahāra
acirāt kṛṣṇa tomāya karibe uddhāra

(*Śrī Caitanya-caritāmṛta, Madhya-līlā* 16.239)

[Within your heart you should keep yourself very faithful, but externally you may behave like an ordinary man. Thus Kṛṣṇa will soon be very pleased and deliver you from the clutches of *māyā*.]

'mane' nija-siddha-deha kariyā bhāvana
rātri-dine kare vraje kṛṣṇera sevana

(*Śrī Caitanya-caritāmṛta, Madhya-līlā* 22.152)

[There are two processes by which one may execute this *rāgānuga-bhakti*: external and internal. When self-realized, the advanced devotee externally remains like a neophyte and executes all the *śāstric* injunctions, especially those concerning hearing and chanting. But within his mind, in his original, purified, self-realized position, he serves Kṛṣṇa in Vṛndāvana in his particular way. He serves Kṛṣṇa twenty-four hours a day, all day and night.]

Here, Śrī Caitanya Mahāprabhujī is saying that in the beginning, one's *niṣṭhā*, firm faith, is to be kept in the core of one's heart, and at the same time one is to behave like an ordinary person in order to sustain one's life. Gradually, when one's faith becomes mature, one's worldly activities will also come to correspond with one's *bhajana*; that is, they will become favorable to *bhajana*. In such a condition, one should meditate on one's internally conceived *siddha-deha*, which is suitable for the service of the Divine Couple, and in the core of one's heart one should mentally serve Them (*aprākṛta mānasī-sevā*). By following this procedure, at first one attains *svarūpa-siddhi*, realization of one's eternal spiritual body. Ultimately, at the stage of *vastu-siddhi* in *prakaṭa* Vraja (the spiritual realm of Vraja which manifests in this world), after giving up the material body, one receives the body of a *gopī* corresponding to one's internally conceived *siddha-deha*.

Mental Speculation

Those giving the *siddha-praṇālī mantra* think, "There can be no auspiciousness for *sādhakas* until they receive *siddha-praṇālī*. There is no necessity for *vaidhī-bhakti sādhana, tattva-jñāna* (knowledge of Reality) or *anartha-nivṛtti* (freedom from thoughts and habits that are unfavorable for advancement in *bhakti*). The *rāgānuga-bhakta* should obtain *siddha-praṇālī* before he goes through *anartha-nivṛtti*. In that way he can avoid getting caught in the inconvenience of *vaidhī-bhakti*." These people's conception is exactly like thinking that a fruit will grow from a leaf before the appearance of a flower.[1]

1 See Endnote 1, at the end of this chapter.

True Sentiments of the Soul

vidhi-mārga-rata-jane, svādhīnatā ratna-dāne,
rāga-mārge karāna praveśa.

(*Śuno, He Rasika Jana*, Verse 4,
by Śrīla Bhaktivinoda Ṭhākura)

[By granting the jewel of independence to those following *vidhi-mārga*, the path of regulative principles, He allows them to enter *rāga-mārga*, the path of spontaneous attachment.]

By considering the gradations of the object of attainment (*sādhya-vastu*), we find that the *prema*, or transcendental love, of Śrīmatī Rādhā for Kṛṣṇa is the crest-jewel. Furthermore, Śrī Caitanya Mahāprabhu has explained that the *sādhya* for the living entities is service to Śrīmatī Rādhikā (*rādhā-dāsya*) imbued with *parakīya-bhāva*, transcendental paramour love. In order to obtain that *sādhya-vastu*, one must perform *sādhana*, the practice of devotional service.

'sādhya-vastu' 'sādhana' vinu keha nāhi pāya
kṛpā kari' kaha, rāya, pābāra upāya

(*Śrī Caitanya-caritāmṛta, Madhya-līlā* 8.197)

[Mahāprabhu inquired: "The goal of life (*sādhya-vastu*) cannot be achieved unless one accepts the appropriate process (*sādhana*). Now, being merciful upon Me, please explain that means by which this goal can be attained."]

In reply to this Śrī Rāya Rāmānanda says,

rādhā-kṛṣṇera līlā ei ati gūḍhatara
dāsya-vātsalyādi-bhāve nā haya gocara

sabe eka sakhī-gaṇera ihāṅ adhikāra
sakhī haite haya ei līlāra vistāra

sakhī vinā ei līlā puṣṭa nāhi haya
sakhī līlā vistāriyā, sakhī āsvādaya

sakhī vinā ei līlāya anyera nāhi gati
sakhī-bhāve ye tāṅre kare anugati

rādhā-kṛṣṇa-kuñjasevā-sādhya sei pāya
sei sādhya pāite āra nāhika upāya

(*Śrī Caitanya-caritāmṛta, Madhya-līlā* 8. 201–205)

ataeva gopī-bhāva kari aṅgīkāra
rātri-dina cinte rādhā-kṛṣṇera vihāra

siddha-dehe cinti' kare tāhāññi sevana
sakhī-bhāve pāya rādhā-kṛṣṇera caraṇa

(*Śrī Caitanya-caritāmṛta, Madhya-līlā* 8. 228–229)

The gist of the matter is that Rādhā-Kṛṣṇa's love-laden *līlā* is so confidential and so full of mysteries that it is imperceptible, even for those in *dāsya-bhāva* and *vātsalya-bhāva*. Only the *sakhīs* are eligible for this. Therefore, no one can attain the service of Śrīmatī Rādhikā or the *kuñja-sevā* of Śrī Rādhā-Kṛṣṇa Yugala by *sādhana* without following in the wake of the *sakhīs*. Thus the only means of attaining this supreme goal is meditation on Rādhā-Kṛṣṇa's pastimes throughout the day and night by the internally conceived *siddha-deha* and in the mood of the *sakhīs*. For this reason, Śrīla Rūpa Gosvāmī has given this instruction in his *Bhakti-rasāmṛta-sindhu* (1.2.294–6), in the section on the *sādhana* of *śrī rāgānuga-bhakti*.

kṛṣṇaṁ smaran janaṁ cāsya preṣṭhaṁ nija-samīhitam
tat-tat-kathā-rataś cāsau kuryād vāsaṁ vraje sadā

sevā sādhaka-rūpeṇa siddha-rūpeṇa cātra hi
tad-bhāva-lipsunā kāryā vraja-lokānusārataḥ

śravaṇotkīrtanādīni vaidha-bhakty-uditāni tu
yāny aṅgāni ca tāny atra vijñeyāni manīṣibhiḥ

[One should always reside in Vraja, remembering Śrī Kṛṣṇa and those dear associates of His whom one aspires to follow, and one should remain engrossed in narrations of their pastimes. If one is unable to reside in Vraja directly, then one should reside in Vraja by mind.

On the path of *rāgānuga*, one should follow Kṛṣṇa's intimate beloved associates and their followers, always remaining absorbed in their service. This should be done by the *sādhaka-rūpa* (the external material body of one's present condition) and also in *siddha-rūpa* (the internally conceived body suitable for rendering the type of service to Śrī Kṛṣṇa for which one's heart is eager). One should eagerly desire the *bhāva* that is the special loving mood of those associates of Kṛṣṇa in Vraja whom one aspires to follow.

Learned scholars who know *bhakti-tattva* point out that in *vaidhī-bhakti* one is instructed to observe the limbs of *bhakti* such as *śravaṇa* (hearing) and *kīrtana* according to one's eligibility. These same instructions also apply in *rāgānuga-bhakti*.]

Here, Śrīla Rūpa Gosvāmī has mentioned two types of *sādhana* in *rāgānuga-bhakti-sevā*:

sevā sādhaka-rūpeṇa siddha-rūpeṇa cātra hi
tad-bhāva-lipsunā kāryā vraja-lokānusārataḥ.

When there is *lobha*, or greed, for *rāgātmikā-bhakti*, *rāgānuga-bhakti* is executed in two ways: in the external body in which one is presently situated (*sādhaka-rūpa*), and in the perfected spiritual form (*siddha-rūpa*). Eagerly desiring to attain *rati* for Kṛṣṇa and the ecstatic sentiments of one's chosen companions of Kṛṣṇa, one must follow the associates of Rādhā and Kṛṣṇa in Vraja, such as Lalitā, Viśākhā, Rūpa Mañjarī, and their followers, such as Śrī Rūpa Gosvāmī and Sanātana Gosvāmī. One must render bodily service with the *sādhaka-rūpa* following the great authorities residing in Vraja, such as Śrī Rūpa and Śrī Sanātana. And with the *siddha-rūpa* one must render *mānasī-sevā* (service to Śrī Śrī Rādhā-Kṛṣṇa performed in the purified mind), following the Vrajavāsīs such as Śrī Rūpa Mañjarī.

The meaning of this verse (*sevā sādhaka-rūpeṇa*) has been explained in *Śrī Caitanya-caritāmṛta* (*Madhya-līlā* 22.156–157):

bāhya, antara,—ihāra dui ta' sādhana
'bāhye' sādhaka-dehe kare śravaṇa-kīrtana

'mane' nija-siddha-deha kariyā bhāvana
rātri-dine kare vraje kṛṣṇera sevana

[This *rāgānuga-bhakti* is performed in two ways: externally and internally. Externally, in the *sādhaka* body, the devotee engages in hearing and chanting. In his mind, in his internally conceived, perfected spiritual body, he serves Kṛṣṇa in Vraja day and night.]

Thus, *rāgānuga-bhakti sādhakas*[2] should in all respects practice *bhāva-sambandhi-sādhana* (those devotional practices that quickly give realization of one's internal spiritual mood), such as *śravaṇa, kīrtana,* service to Tulasī, wearing *tilaka,* observing vows beginning with Śrī Ekādaśī and Janmāṣṭamī, and so on, for all these activities nourish one's intrinsic desired *bhāva.* Simultaneously, one must also render service to Rādhā-Kṛṣṇa in Vraja, meditating on one's *siddha-deha* in the heart. The body of a *gopī,* which is suitable for rendering service to Rādhā-Govinda, is called *siddha-deha.* When *bhajana* is mature, the living entity gives up his inert material body and attains the body of a *gopī* corresponding to its eternal intrinsic nature.

In *Śrī Prema-bhakti-candrika* (5.8) Śrīla Narottama Ṭhākura has said: "*sādhane bhābiba jāhā siddha-dehe pāba tāhā, rāga pathera ei se upāya* – whatever subject is constantly meditated upon at the time of performing one's spiritual practice

2 See Endnote 2, at the end of this chapter.

(*sādhana*), that same subject is the prominent meditation at the time of death and it engrosses the heart." One's destination at the time of death will correspond exactly to the subject one remembers at that time. At the time of death, the saintly King Bhārata was immersed in thinking about a baby deer, and therefore he attained the body of a deer, so what doubt is there about attaining the body suitable for rendering to the Divine Couple the service on which one constantly reflected in one's internally conceived *siddha-deha*?

In relation to the *siddha-deha*, it has been said in the *Śrī Sanat-Kumāra Saṁhitā* (184, 186):

ātmānaṁ cintayet tatra tāsāṁ madhye manoramām
rūpayauvanasampannāṁ kiśorīṁ premodāakṛtim

rādhikānuñcarī nityaṁ tat sevana parāyaṇāṁ
kṛṣṇād apy adhikaṁ prema rādhikāyāṁ prakurvatīm

(Sadāśiva is explaining to Nāradajī about the *siddha-deha* suitable for rendering service to the Divine Couple.) "O Nārada, meditate in this way upon your own *svarūpa* (constitutional spiritual form) among Śrī Kṛṣṇa's beloved associates who take pride in being His paramours in *aprākṛta* (transcendental) Vṛndāvana-dhāma. 'I am a most beautiful and supremely blissful *kiśorī*, an adolescent girl, endowed with youthful beauty. I am an eternal maidservant of Śrīmatī Rādhikā. Having arranged for Śrī Kṛṣṇa's dear-most sweetheart, Śrīmatī Rādhikā, to meet with Him, I will always strive for Their happiness. Remaining forever engaged in the service of the Divine Couple, may I maintain more love for Śrīmatī than for Kṛṣṇa.'"

We should note that the descriptions of the *siddha-deha* that *śāstra* and the *mahājanas* have given are for *sādhakas* of a particular level. Any mention of the *siddha-deha* is always in the context of *rāgānuga-bhakti*. Specifically, such instructions are intended for those fortunate *sādhakas* in whose hearts *lobha*, a genuine greed, to attain *rāgātmika-bhakti* has already arisen due to impressions (*saṁskāras*) from this life and previous lives.

There is a further matter to consider. It is one thing to understand the excellence of a particular *rasa*, or transcendental mellow, by the description given in *śāstra*. It is another thing altogether to have greed (*lobha*) for that *rasa*. When someone has *lobha* for a particular *rasa*, that *sādhaka* will exhibit its symptoms. Such greed arises in the stage of *ruci*, and this marks the beginning of the practice of *rāgānuga-bhakti*. It is understood from this that *nāma-aparādha*, *sevā-aparādhā* (offenses committed whilst performing service), and various other *anarthas* of a *sādhaka* have, for the most part, been eradicated by now.

He has already controlled the six urges mentioned by Śrīla Rūpa Gosvāmī in *Śrī Upadeśāmṛta* (Verse 1); he is virtually free from the six faults (Verse 2); he is endowed with the six qualities beginning with enthusiasm and confidence (Verse 3); having recognized the three types of Vaiṣṇavas, he is expert in behaving appropriately with them (Verse 5); and he has also become established in the purport of Verse 8, *tan-nāma-rūpa-caritādi*. In other words, he conducts himself according to this verse.

In this stage the *sādhaka* goes on performing *bhajana*, and when he crosses the stage of *ruci* and enters *āśakti*, then a semblance of the symptoms related by Śrī Rūpa Gosvāmī in the verse *kṣāntir-avyartha-kālatvaṁ* will be observed in him. In the stage of *āśakti*, a semblance (*ābhāsa*) of the *rati* that arises in the stage of *bhāva* will appear, and in order to manifest that *rati* fully, the *sādhaka* will perform *bhajana*, meditating on his *siddha-deha*. When this *ratyābhāsa*, or semblance of *rati* (*bhāva-bhakti*), transforms into *rati* by the practice of *bhajana*, then the *sādhaka* attains factual experience of his *svarūpa*.

This is called meditation on *siddha-deha*, or the acceptance of *vaiṣṇava-bheka*. One who achieves this, being of simple heart, is worshipful for the whole world.

Śrīla Bhaktivinoda Ṭhākura's Perfection

Śrīla Bhaktivinoda Ṭhākura has described his eternal spiritual form (*siddha-svarūpa*) in one of his songs (*Gīta-mālā*, Chapter 5, Song 8):

varaṅe taḍit vāsa tārāvalī kamala maṇjarī nāma
sāḍe bāra varṣa vayasa satata svānanda sukhada dhāma

karpūra sevā lalitāra gaṅa rādhā yūtheśvarī hana
mameśvarī-nātha śrī nanda-nandana āmāra parāṅa dhana

śrī rūpa maṇjarī prabhṛtira sama yugala sevāya āśa
avaśya se-rūpa sevā pāba āmi parākāṣṭhā suviśvāsa

kabe bā e dāsī saṁsiddhi labhibe rādhā-kuṅḍe vāsa kari'
rādhā-kṛṣṇa sevā satata karibe pūrva smṛti parihari'

[My complexion is like a flash of lightning and my dress is bedecked with twinkling stars. My name is Kamala Mañjarī, and I am eternally twelve-and-a-half years old. My home is Svānanda-sukhada-kuñja. My service is to supply camphor to the Divine Couple. I serve in Lalitā's group (*gaṇa*), and Śrī Rādhā is my group leader (*yūtheśvarī*). My Svāminī's beloved, the son of Nanda Mahārāja, is the treasure of my life. I aspire to serve the Divine Couple like Rūpa Mañjarī and others, and I am confident that I will surely attain this service. This is my highest aspiration. Oh, when will this maidservant attain complete perfection and, residing at Śrī Rādhā-kuṇḍa, serve Śrī Śrī Rādhā-Kṛṣṇa in complete forgetfulness of my past?]

Endnotes

1 An excerpt from a conversation with Śrīla Bhaktivedānta Svāmī Mahārāja in New Vṛndāvana, on June 23, 1976:

Śrīla Prabhupāda: ...Your business is to cure yourself. *Anartha-nivṛtti*, that is *anartha-nivṛtti*. Then *svarūpa* will come. That is the *bābājīs*. In Vṛndāvana, you have seen? *Siddha-praṇālī*.

Pradyumna: *Siddha-praṇālī*, *siddha-deha*?

Śrīla Prabhupāda: They are smoking and having illicit sex with one dozen women – [and they call that] *svarūpa*. Rascal. This is called *sahajiyā*, a rascal. Condemned. Where is your *svarūpa*? Don't talk unnecessarily. First of all come to *svarūpa*, then talk of *svarūpa*.

An excerpt from a conversation with Śrīla Bhaktivedānta Svāmī Mahārāja in Los Angeles on June 7, 1976:

Śrīla Prabhupāda: Then everything will be finished. Preaching will be finished. In this *sahajiyā* party, then preaching will be finished. *Siddha-praṇālī*.

Tamāla Kṛṣṇa: What does that mean, Śrīla Prabhupāda, *siddha-praṇālī*?

Śrīla Prabhupāda: [Their] *siddha-praṇālī* is nonsense. They have manufactured a *siddha-praṇālī*.

Rāmeśvara: (break) ...the initiation that you are given your *siddha*, your eternal position.

Tamāla Kṛṣṇa: There are some very strange notes...

Śrīla Prabhupāda: They have learned it from these Rādhā-kuṇḍa *bābājīs*... They're fools, rascals, so whatever they say...

Rāmeśvara: The dangerous thing is that they are using your book for authority.

Śrīla Prabhupāda: ...Authority, where? ...That I've already explained. Why these rascals do not take the lessons of Caitanya Mahāprabhu that we are all rascals, fools? No. That they will not take. They'll take Rādhārāṇī's *bhāva*. What Caitanya Mahāprabhu is teaching by His practical life, that we have to take.

Rāmeśvara: There is one statement, Śrīla Prabhupāda, regarding devotional service in a reverential mood. So they have found some quote, they are quoting, that this reverential devotional service is an impediment towards developing pure love.

Tamāla Kṛṣṇa: Another place they quote that regulative principles are a hindrance on the path... There's a statement somewhere in one of your books that when one attains the highest platform...

Śrīla Prabhupāda: Then where is that highest platform?

Tamāla Kṛṣṇa: Yes, there's no question of it.

Rāmeśvara: One must go through stages.

Śrīla Prabhupāda: Yes.

Rāmeśvara: You gave the example of trying to get an M. A. degree.

Śrīla Prabhupāda: Yes. One has to come to that highest stage. It is not forbidden. That may be ideal, but not for the neophytes. You must... One who does not know ABCD, what he will know about M. A. degrees? That they do not know. They think that they have already passed M. A. degree. That is their fault.

Tamāla Kṛṣṇa: There's another statement, I saw them, where it says, it's a quote, that you can treat Kṛṣṇa as your lover and Kṛṣṇa will reciprocate.

Hari-śauri: And they underlined the two words "you can" treat Kṛṣṇa as your lover. In this way they're taking your quotes out of context.

Rāmeśvara: This is one of their main, the main ideas in their philosophy is that the living entity can desire to have any relationship he wants with Kṛṣṇa.

Śrīla Prabhupāda: That is all right, he can desire. I already explained: first deserve, then desire... You are rascal, how you can desire? You have no qualification; you desire to be a high court judge. What is this nonsense?

Rāmeśvara: But then they have an answer.

Śrīla Prabhupāda: What is that answer?

Rāmeśvara: That, "Let me just try it anyway, to keep my mind thinking..."

Śrīla Prabhupāda: How you can try it? First of all, be qualified, a big lawyer. Then you become high court judge. Where is that qualification? You are after illicit sex and *bīḍīs*, and you want to be associated with the *gopīs*.

2 Excerpts from *Śrī Caitanya-caritāmṛta, Madhya-līlā* 22, on *rāgānuga-bhakti*:

"The original inhabitants of Vṛndāvana are attached to Kṛṣṇa spontaneously in devotional service. Nothing can compare to such spontaneous devotional service, which is called *rāgātmika-bhakti*. When a devotee follows in the footsteps of the devotees of Vṛndāvana, his devotional service is called *rāgānuga-bhakti*"* (*Śrī Caitanya-caritāmṛta, Madhya-līlā* 22.149).

"When one becomes attached to the Supreme Personality of Godhead, his natural inclination to love is fully absorbed in thoughts of the Lord. That is called transcendental attachment, and devotional service according to that attachment is called *rāgātmikā*, or spontaneous devotional service"* (*Śrī Caitanya-caritāmṛta, Madhya-līlā* 22.150).

"Thus, devotional service which consists of *rāga* [deep attachment] is called *rāgātmikā*, spontaneous loving service. If a devotee covets such a position, he is considered to be most fortunate"* (*Śrī Caitanya-caritāmṛta, Madhya-līlā* 22.152).

"If one follows in the footsteps of the inhabitants of Vṛndāvana out of such transcendental covetousness, he does not care for the injunctions or reasonings of *śāstra*. That is the way of spontaneous love"* (*Śrī Caitanya-caritāmṛta, Madhya-līlā* 22.153).

An excerpt from a lecture on *Śrīmad-Bhāgavatam* by Śrīla Bhaktivedānta Svāmī Mahārāja, spoken in Vṛndāvana on November 12, 1972:

So you have to uncover. You have to discover. That discovering process is devotional service. The more you are engaged in devotional service, the more your senses become pure or uncovered. And when it is completely uncovered, without any designation, then you are capable to serve Kṛṣṇa.

This is apprenticeship, *vaidhī-bhakti* (devotion prompted by the regulations of the scriptures); that is apprenticeship. Real *bhakti, para-bhakti,* that is *rāgānuga-bhakti.* This *rāgānuga-bhakti,* we have to come to it after surpassing the *vaidhī-bhakti.* In the material world, if we do not try to make further and further progress in devotional service, if we are simply sticking to the *śāstric* regulation process and do not try to go beyond that. [...]

Śāstric process is regulation. That is required. Without *śāstric* process you cannot go to that platform. But if we stick to the *śāstric* process only and do not try to improve ourselves. [...] The *śāstric* process is *kaniṣṭha-adhikara,* lowest stage of devotional service.

An excerpt Śrīla Bhaktivedānta Nārāyaṇa Gosvāmī Mahārāja's commentary on *Bhajana-rahasya,* Chapter 7, Text 6:

There are five kinds of *sādhana* in *rāgānuga-bhakti*:

(1) *Svābhīṣṭa-bhāvamaya* (composed of one's desired mood): When *śravaṇa* (hearing), *kīrtana,* and other such limbs of *bhakti* are saturated with one of the primary *bhāvas* (*dāsya,* servitude; *sakhya,* friendship; *vātsalya,* paternal affection; or *mādhurya,* conjugal), they nourish the tree of the *sādhaka's* future *prema.* At that time they are called *bhāvamaya-sādhana.* When *prema,* transcendental love, manifests, they are called *bhāvamaya-sādhya.*

(2) *Svābhīṣṭa-bhāva-sambandhī* (related to one's desired mood): The limbs of *bhakti*, including *śrī-guru-padāśraya* (service to *śrī guru*), *mantra-japa* (chanting the holy names), *smaraṇa* (remembrance), *dhyāna* (meditation), and so on, are known as *bhāva-sambandhī-sādhana*. Because the following of vows on holy days such as Ekādaśī and Janmāṣṭamī assists the limb of *smaraṇa*, it is considered partial *bhāva-sambandhī*.

(3) *Svābhīṣṭa-bhāva-anukūla* (favorable to one's desired mood): Wearing neck beads made of *tulasī*, applying *tilaka*[3], adopting the outward signs of a Vaiṣṇava, rendering *tulasī-sevā*[4], performing *parikramā* (circumambulating the holy places), offering *praṇāma* (obeisances), and so forth are *bhāva-anukūla*.

(4) *Svābhīṣṭa-bhāva-aviruddha* (neither opposed to nor incompatible with one's desired mood): Respecting cows, the *banyan* tree, the *myrobalan* tree, and *brāhmaṇas* (priests or teachers of divine knowledge) are conducive limbs and are therefore called *bhāva-aviruddha*.

The above-mentioned (1–4) kinds of *sādhana* are all to be adopted in the performance of *bhajana*.

(5) *Svābhīṣṭa-bhāva-viruddha* (opposed to one's desired mood): *Nyāsa* (mental assignment of different parts of the body to various deities), *mudrā* (particular positions of intertwining the fingers), *dvārakā-dhyāna* (meditation on Śrī Kṛṣṇa's pastimes in Dvārakā), and other such limbs should be abandoned in the performance of *rāgānuga-bhakti* because they are opposed to the attainment of one's desired *bhāva*.

---

3 *Tilaka* is the vertical clay markings of the Vaiṣṇavas, worn on the forehead and other parts of the body to symbolize their devotion to Lord Kṛṣṇa or Viṣṇu.

4 *Tulasī* is a sacred plant whose leaves and blossoms are used by Vaiṣṇavas in the worship of Śrī Kṛṣṇa; a partial expansion of Vṛndā-devī. The wood is also used for chanting beads and neck beads.

Conclusion

[An excerpt from Śrīla Bhaktivedānta Nārāyaṇa Gosvāmī Mahārāja's commentary on *Bhajana-rahasya*, Chapter 6, Text 6:]

In pure, transcendental nature, Śrī Kṛṣṇa is the only male and all *jīvas* are female. Actually, in the structure of the *jīva's* heart, male and female characteristics do not exist; yet, when embodied, the living entity naturally conceives of itself as being male or female. The *jīva* attains a pure body through the medium of *sādhana-bhajana*. A person who is inclined towards the amorous mellow (*mādhurya-rasa*) will perform *sādhana-bhajana* under the guidance of *rasika-bhaktas* and, according to his own desire and constitutional nature, he will attain his spiritual form, which will be the body of a *gopī*. Yogamāyā makes all arrangements for the devotee's service in a specific *rasa* by the potency that makes the impossible possible (*aghaṭana-ghaṭana-paṭīyasī-śakti*).

Appendix

ISKCON Means Gauḍīya Vaiṣṇavism

[The following is an excerpt from Śrīla Bhaktivedānta Nārāyaṇa Gosvāmī Mahārāja's lecture in Varṣāṇa, India, on November 20, 2001, on the occasion of Śrīla Bhaktivedānta Svāmī Mahārāja's disappearance day.]

ISKCON: From The Beginning of Creation

Śrīla Nārāyaṇa Gosvāmī Mahārāja: I want to clarify something. We hear and read that Śrīla Bhaktivedānta Svāmī Mahārāja established ISKCON (International Society for Kṛṣṇa Consciousness). What is ISKCON? He himself has clarified the meaning, beginning with *kṛṣṇah-bhakti-rasa-bhāvitā-matiḥ* [*Śrī Caitanya-caritāmṛta, Madhya-līlā* 8.70].[1] Those who follow this verse are actually ISKCON members. ISKCON is not new.

---

1 Śrīla Prabhupāda states in *The Journey of Self Discovery*: "I have translated the words 'Kṛṣṇa consciousness' from *kṛṣṇa-bhakti-rasa-bhāvitā*."
Śrī Caitanya-caritāmṛta, Madhya-līlā 8.70: "*kṛṣṇa-bhakti-rasa-bhāvitā matiḥ krīyatāṁ yadi kuto 'pi labhyate tatra laulyam api mūlyam ekalaṁ janma-koṭi-sukṛtair na labhyate* – Pure devotional service in Kṛṣṇa consciousness cannot be had even by pious activities in hundreds and thousands of lives. It can be obtained only by paying one price; that is, intense greed to obtain it. If it is available somewhere, one must purchase it without delay."*

Your Prabhupāda did not actually establish ISKCON. ISKCON was established by Brahmā, and by Kṛṣṇa Himself. Brahmā is one of the four *sampradāya gurus*, and he established ISKCON by the mercy of Kṛṣṇa. Nārada is the first ISKCON member, Śrīla Vyāsadeva is the second, and Śrī Sukadeva Gosvāmī is the third. All pure devotees in the *guru-paramparā* are ISKCON members.[2]

Śrīla Svāmī Mahārāja translated the name ISKCON into English, but Vaiṣṇava society has actually existed since the origin of creation, the beginning of time. As he himself has said, it is "the same wine in a new bottle." He never created anything new. He gave the same philosophy that Kṛṣṇa gave in His *Gītā*, the same philosophy that was given by Śrīla Vyāsadeva in his *Śrīmad-Bhāgavatam*, and the same philosophy that was given by Kṛṣṇadāsa Kavirāja Gosvāmī in *Śrī Caitanya-caritāmṛta*. He took all these teachings from his *guru*, Śrīla Bhaktisiddhānta Sarasvatī Gosvāmī Ṭhākura, and he also took something from his *sannyāsa guru*, Śrīla Bhakti Prajñāna Keśava Gosvāmī Mahārāja. He received the *sannyāsa mantra* from him, the *mantra* for attaining the service of Rādhā, and after that he preached this mission. In this way, only the name of his mission was new, and it was mainly only new to Western countries. In India ISKCON has been extant from the beginning of time.

---

2 An excerpt from Śrīla Bhaktivedānta Svāmī Mahārāja's lecture on December 1, 1966: "I have given you the process of disciplic succession: from Kṛṣṇa, Brahmā; from Brahmā, Nārada; from Nārada, Vyāsa; from Vyāsa, Madhva; from Madhva, Mādhavendra Puri; from Mādhavendra Purī, Īśvara Purī; from Isvara Purī, Lord Caitanya. So, *evam paramparā*. In the *paramparā* system, in that disciplic succession, you will find no change... They are not foolish to manufacture something new... If you want the real thing, then you have to take the old – the oldest. You cannot change anything. Can you change the law of the sun rising or setting? The old laws are going on, and you have to follow them."

Gauḍīya Sannyāsīs Never Become Bābājīs

[During his lecture Śrīla Gurudeva noticed a guest in the audience who had received *sannyāsa* from Śrīla Bhaktivedānta Svāmī Mahārāja Prabhupāda, and after Prabhupāda's disappearance took *bābājī-veśa*. He then commented:]

Śrīla Nārāyaṇa Gosvāmī Mahārāja: I have not seen any instance that a devotee who took *sannyāsa* from Śrīla Prabhupāda Bhaktisiddhānta Sarasvatī Ṭhākura has taken *bābājī-veśa*. There is no example at all.

Guest: What about Kṛṣṇa dāsa Bābājī? "

Śrīla Nārāyaṇa Gosvāmī Mahārāja: Kṛṣṇa dāsa Bābājī was not a direct disciple of Śrīla Prabhupāda Sarasvatī Ṭhākura. My Guru Mahārāja never accepted him as a *bābājī*. He always addressed him by his *brahmacārī* name, Svādhikārānanda Brahmacārī. Kṛṣṇa dāsa Bābājī had not previously accepted Śrīla Prabhupāda as his *sannyāsa-guru*, and moreover he had never been a *sannyāsi*. He had been a *brahmacārī*.

There is no example in the entire history of Śrīla Sarasvatī Ṭhākura Prabhupāda's *sannyāsīs* that anyone has given up his *sannyāsa* dress and taken the dress of a *bābājī*. The proper conceptions and principles of *sannyāsa* are in line with the principles of ISKCON. We are also ISKCON, and we will be ISKCON forever. One who is actually a member of ISKCON will never leave ISKCON, in this life or any future life.

Guest: Śrīla Purī Mahārāja gave *bābājī-veśa* to some disciples.

Śrīla Nārāyaṇa Gosvāmī Mahārāja: We are not speaking about giving *bābājī-veśa*. He never gave *bābājī-veśa* to anyone who was previously given *sannyāsa*. Our Guru Mahārāja also gave *bābājī-veśa*, and Śrīla Prabhupāda Bhaktisiddhānta Sarasvatī Ṭhākura also gave *bābājī-veśa* to some, but they never changed anyone from *sannyāsa* to *bābājī*.

There is almost no difference between a *sannyāsī* and *bābājī*, in the sense that the *mantra* of both is the same. The main difference is that the *bābājī* is mostly a *bhajanānandī* (a renunciant who mostly concentrates on his personal *bhajana*, spending less time in preaching activities), and the *sannyāsī* is a *goṣṭhyānandī* (a preacher who is also engaged in *bhajana*). Only those who don't know the principles of either can change their dress. We should not change.

Appendix

Dangers of Imitation

From the Books and Discourses of Śrī Śrīmad Bhaktivedānta Svāmī Mahārāja

[In Part III of this book, Śrīla Nārāyaṇa Gosvāmī Mahārāja glorifies Śrīla Bhaktivedānta Svāmī Mahārāja for establishing the principles of pure *bhakti* throughout the world. We are therefore pleased to share with you some excerpts from his books and discourses on the subject of discerning the true sentiments of the soul and the soul's relationship with the Supreme Soul, Śrī Śrī Rādhā-Kṛṣṇa.

In the last section, called *The Gopīs' Greatness*, we have inserted two excerpts from the discourses of Śrīla Nārāyaṇa Gosvāmī Mahārāja to further clarify and expand upon the points made by Śrīla Bhaktivedānta Svāmī Mahārāja.]

A Vain Attempt

An excerpt from *Śrī Caitanya-caritāmṛta*, Introduction

Lord Caitanya gives a practical demonstration of how to love God in the conjugal relationship. Taking the part of Rādhārāṇī, Caitanya tries to love Kṛṣṇa as Rādhārāṇī loved Him. Kṛṣṇa was always amazed by Rādhārāṇī's love. He would ask, "How does Rādhārāṇī give Me such pleasure?" In order to study Rādhārāṇī, Kṛṣṇa lived in Her role and tried to understand Himself. This is the secret of Lord Caitanya's incarnation. Caitanya is Kṛṣṇa, but He has taken the mood or role of Rādhārāṇī to show us how to love Kṛṣṇa. Thus He is addressed: "I offer my respectful obeisances unto the Supreme Lord who is absorbed in Rādhārāṇī's thoughts."

This brings up the question of who is Rādhārāṇī and what is Rādhā-Kṛṣṇa. Actually, Rādhā-Kṛṣṇa is the exchange of love. This is not ordinary love. Kṛṣṇa has immense potencies, of which three are principal: internal, external and marginal. In the internal potency there are three divisions: *samvit, hlādinī* and *sandhinī* (knowledge, bliss, and eternity). The *hlādinī* potency is Kṛṣṇa's pleasure potency. All living entities have this pleasure-seeking potency, for all beings are trying to have pleasure. This is the very nature of the living entity. At present we are trying to enjoy our pleasure potency by means of the body in the material condition. By bodily contact we are attempting to derive pleasure from material sense objects.

But we should not entertain the nonsensical idea that Kṛṣṇa, who is always spiritual, also tries to seek pleasure on this material plane. In the *Bhagavad-gītā* Kṛṣṇa describes the material universe as a nonpermanent place full of miseries. Why, then, would He seek pleasure in matter? He is the Supersoul, the Supreme Spirit, and His pleasure is beyond the material conception.

To learn how Kṛṣṇa enjoys pleasure, we must study the first nine cantos of *Śrīmad-Bhāgavatam*, and then we should study the Tenth Canto, in which Kṛṣṇa's pleasure potency is displayed in His pastimes with Rādhārāṇī and the damsels of Vraja. Unfortunately, unintelligent people turn at once to the sports of Kṛṣṇa in the *Daśama-skandha*, the Tenth Canto. Kṛṣṇa's embracing Rādhārāṇī or His dancing with the cowherd girls in the *rāsa* dance are generally not understood by ordinary men, because they consider these pastimes in the light of mundane lust. They foolishly think that Kṛṣṇa is like themselves and that He embraces the *gopīs* just as an ordinary man embraces a young girl. Some people thus become interested in Kṛṣṇa because they think that His religion allows indulgence in sex. This is not *kṛṣṇa-bhakti*, love of Kṛṣṇa, but *prākṛta-sahajiyā* – materialistic lust. [...] Kṛṣṇa, however, does not make such a vain attempt.

A Class of So-called Devotees

Excerpts from *Śrī Caitanya-caritāmṛta, Ādi-līlā* 4.34, 35, 41

anugrahāya bhaktānāṁ
mānuṣaṁ deham āsthitaḥ
bhajate tādṛśīḥ krīḍa
yāḥ śrutvā tat-paro bhavet
(*Śrī Caitanya-caritāmṛta, Ādi-līlā* 4.34)

Kṛṣṇa manifests His eternal humanlike form and performs His pastimes to show mercy to the devotees. Having heard such pastimes, one should engage in service to Him.

PURPORT

This text is from *Śrīmad-Bhāgavatam* (10.33.36). The Supreme Personality of Godhead has innumerable expansions of His transcendental form who eternally exist in the spiritual world. This material world is only a perverted reflection of the spiritual world, where everything is manifested without inebriety. There everything is in its original existence, free from the domination of time. Time cannot deteriorate or interfere with the conditions in the spiritual world, where different manifestations of the Supreme Personality of Godhead are the recipients of the worship of different living entities in their constitutional spiritual positions. In the spiritual world all existence is unadulterated goodness. The goodness found in the material world is contaminated by the modes of passion and ignorance.

[...] Special natural appreciation of the descriptions of a particular pastime of Godhead indicates the constitutional position of a living entity. Adoration, servitorship, friendship, parental affection, and conjugal love are the five primary relationships with Kṛṣṇa. The highest perfectional stage of the conjugal relationship, enriched by many sentiments, gives the maximum relishable mellow to the devotee.

The Lord appears in different incarnations – as a fish, tortoise and boar, as Paraśurāma, Lord Rāma, Buddha, and so on – to reciprocate the different appreciations of living entities in different stages of evolution. The conjugal relationship of amorous love called *parakīya-rasa* is the unparalleled perfection of love exhibited by Lord Kṛṣṇa and His devotees.

[...] Materialistic conditioned souls do not understand the transcendental exchanges of love, but they like to indulge in sense gratification in the name of devotional service. The activities of the Supreme Lord can never be understood by irresponsible persons who think the pastimes of Rādhā and Kṛṣṇa to be ordinary affairs. The *rāsa* dance is arranged by Kṛṣṇa's internal potency *yogamāyā*, and it is beyond the grasp of the materially affected person. Trying to throw mud into transcendence with their perversity, the *sahajiyās* misinterpret the sayings *tat-paratvena nirmalam* [*Śrī Caitanya-caritāmṛta, Madhya-līlā* 19.170] and *tat-paro bhavet*. By misinterpreting *tādṛśīḥ krīḍāḥ*, they want to indulge in sex while pretending to imitate Lord Kṛṣṇa. But one must actually understand the imports of the words through the intelligence of the authorized *gosvāmīs*. Śrīla Narottama dāsa Ṭhākura, in his prayers to the Gosvāmīs, has explained his inability to understand such spiritual affairs:

rūpa-raghunātha-pade ha-ibe ākuti
kabe hāma bujhaba se yugala-pīriti

(*Gaurāṅga Bolite Habe,* Verse 4)

When I shall be eager to understand the literature given by the Gosvāmīs, then I shall be able to understand the transcendental love affairs of Rādhā and Kṛṣṇa.

In other words, unless one is trained under the disciplic succession of the Gosvāmīs, one cannot understand Rādhā and Kṛṣṇa. The conditioned souls are naturally averse to understanding the spiritual existence of the Lord, and if they try to know the transcendental nature of the Lord's pastimes while they remain absorbed in materialism, they are sure to blunder like the *sahajiyās.*

****

'bhavet' kriyā vidhiliṅ, sei ihā kaya
kartavya avaśya ei, anyathā pratyavāya

(*Śrī Caitanya-caritāmṛta, Ādi-līlā* 4.35)

Here the use of the verb *bhavet,* which is in the imperative mood, tells us that this certainly must be done. Noncompliance would be abandonment of duty.

PURPORT

This imperative is applicable to pure devotees. Neophytes will be able to understand these affairs only after being elevated by regulated devotional service under the expert guidance of the spiritual master. Then they too will be competent to hear of the love affairs of Rādhā and Kṛṣṇa.

As long as one is in material, conditioned life, strict discipline is required in the matter of moral and immoral activities.

The absolute world is transcendental and free from such distinctions because there inebriety is not possible. But in this material world a sexual appetite necessitates distinction between moral and immoral conduct. There are no sexual activities in the spiritual world. The transactions between lover and beloved in the spiritual world are pure transcendental love and unadulterated bliss.

One who has not been attracted by the transcendental beauty of *rasa* will certainly be dragged down into material attraction, thus to act in material contamination and progress to the darkest region of hellish life. But by understanding the conjugal love of Rādhā and Kṛṣṇa one is freed from the grip of attraction to material so-called love between man and woman. Similarly, one who understands the pure parental love of Nanda and Yaśodā for Kṛṣṇa will be saved from being dragged into material parental affection. If one accepts Kṛṣṇa as the supreme friend, the attraction of material friendship will be finished for him, and he will not be dismayed by so-called friendship with mundane wranglers. If he is attracted by servitorship to Kṛṣṇa, he will no longer have to serve the material body in the degraded status of material existence, with the false hope of becoming master in the future. Similarly, one who sees the greatness of Kṛṣṇa in neutrality will certainly never again seek the so-called relief of impersonalist or voidist philosophy.

If one is not attracted by the transcendental nature of Kṛṣṇa, one is sure to be attracted to material enjoyment, thus to become implicated in the clinging network of virtuous and sinful activities and to continue material existence by transmigrating from one material body to another. Only in Kṛṣṇa consciousness can one achieve the highest perfection of life. [...]

****

ei-mata bhakta-bhāva kari' aṅgīkāra
āpani ācari' bhakti karila pracāra

(*Śrī Caitanya-caritāmṛta, Ādi-līlā* 4.41)

In this way, assuming the sentiment of a devotee, He preached devotional service while practicing it Himself.

PURPORT

[...] Svarūpa Dāmodara Gosvāmī has described Lord Caitanya as Kṛṣṇa Himself with the attitude of Rādhārāṇī, or a combination of Rādhā and Kṛṣṇa. The intention of Lord Caitanya is to taste Kṛṣṇa's sweetness in transcendental love. He does not care to think of Himself as Kṛṣṇa, because He wants the position of Rādhārāṇī.

We should remember this. A class of so-called devotees called the *nadīyā-nāgarīs* or *gaura-nāgarīs* pretend that they have the sentiment of *gopīs* toward Lord Caitanya, but they do not realize that He placed Himself not as the enjoyer, Kṛṣṇa, but as the enjoyed, the devotee of Kṛṣṇa. The concoctions of unauthorized persons pretending to be bona fide have not been accepted by Lord Caitanya. Presentations such as those of the *gaura-nāgarīs* are only disturbances to the sincere execution of the mission of Lord Caitanya.

A Mistake

An excerpt from a lecture spoken in Māyāpura, India, on February 10, 1977

Kṛṣṇa says personally, and Vedānta says, "*janmādy asya yataḥ* – Absolute Truth is that from where everything is coming." So the lust is also coming from Kṛṣṇa. We find lusty desire among the *gopīs*, among Kṛṣṇa, but Kṛṣṇa-Caitanya Mahāprabhu recommends, "*ramya kācid upāsana vrajavadhū vargena ya kalpitā* – There is no better mode of worship than it was conceived by the *vrajavadhū*, damsels of Vraja, Vṛndāvana; *parakīya-rasa*." But in the material world, Caitanya Mahāprabhu was so strict about woman that once upon a time there was the singing of a woman in the Jagannātha temple, and Caitanya Mahāprabhu was running fast, thinking, "Oh, what nice singing is going on in the temple. Let Me go and hear." But Govinda, His personal servant, checked Him: "My dear Sir, this singing is done by a woman." "Oh? It is a woman? Govinda, you have saved My life."

Just see. And the same Caitanya Mahāprabhu has recommended about the *gopīs* who loved Kṛṣṇa as paramour: *ramya kācid upāsana vrajavadhū-vargena ya kalpitā*. Just see the distinction. The same business is there, but it is all spiritual. [...] It looks similar, but it is not the same thing. One is gold, one is iron. A polished iron, a golden thing, of golden color, does not mean it is gold. "All that glitters is not gold."

The Gopīs' Greatness

An excerpt from *Kṛṣṇa, The Supreme Personality of Godhead*, Chapter 33

As pure devotees, the more the *gopīs* enjoyed Kṛṣṇa's company, the more they became enlightened with His glories, and thus they reciprocated with Him. They wanted to satisfy Kṛṣṇa by glorifying His transcendental pastimes.

> [He [Arjuna] saw an old lady sitting on the river's bank, a spiritual effulgence emanating from her body. Her hair was totally white and she was in *samādhi*. One could not say how old she was.
>
> Arjuna offered her his obeisances, and she came to her external consciousness. Arjuna asked who she was and what she was doing there. She replied that

she had been meditating upon Kṛṣṇa for thousands of years.

By Kṛṣṇa's mercy, Arjuna was able to see her; otherwise no one could see her. Arjuna asked why she was meditating upon Kṛṣṇa. In reply, she said that she had seen the moods of the *gopīs*, and understood that Kṛṣṇa can become subservient to their love alone. The *gopīs* had given up their families, society, chastity, *dharma*, and so on to serve Kṛṣṇa, and He thus always remains indebted to them. She was therefore meditating and desiring to be born from the womb of a *gopī*. She wanted to become the *gopīs'* servant, in order to assist in their service to the divine couple Śrī Śrī Rādhā-Kṛṣṇa. Arjuna was astonished and asked who she was. She replied that she was a *veda-mantra* of one of the branches of the Upaniṣads.][3]

In order to clear up further misconceptions about the *rāsa* dance and the affairs of Kṛṣṇa and the *gopīs*, Mahārāja Parīkṣit, the hearer of *Śrīmad-Bhāgavatam*, told Śukadeva Gosvāmī, "Kṛṣṇa appeared on the earth to establish the regulative principles of religion and to curb the predominance of irreligion. But the behavior of Kṛṣṇa and the *gopīs* might encourage irreligious principles in the material world. I am simply surprised that He would act in such a way, enjoying the company of others' wives in the dead of night."

The basic Vedic injunctions never allow a person to enjoy sex with any woman except his own wife. Kṛṣṇa's appreciation of the *gopīs* appeared to be distinctly in violation of these rules. Mahārāja Parīkṣit understood the total situation from Śukadeva Gosvāmī, yet to further clarify the transcendental nature of Kṛṣṇa and the *gopīs* in the *rāsa* dance, he expressed

3 This insertion is an excerpt from a lecture by Śrīla Bhaktivedānta Nārāyaṇa Gosvāmī Mahārāja, spoken in New Zealand on January 30, 2002.

his surprise. This is very important in order to check the unrestricted association with women by the *prākṛta-sahajiyās.*

Some may take it for granted that Kṛṣṇa was very lusty among young girls, but Parīkṣit Mahārāja said that this was not possible. He could not be lusty. First of all, from the material calculation He was only eight years old. At that age a boy cannot be lusty. *Āptakāma* means that the Supreme Personality of Godhead is self-satisfied. Even if He were lusty, He doesn't need to take help from others to satisfy His lusty desires. The next point is that, although not lusty Himself, He might have been seduced by the lusty desires of the *gopīs.* But Mahārāja Parīkṣit then used another word, *yadu-pati,* which indicates that Kṛṣṇa is the most exalted personality in the dynasty of the Yadus. The kings in the dynasty of Yadu were considered to be the most pious, and their descendants were also like that. Having taken birth in that family, how could Kṛṣṇa have been seduced, even by the *gopīs*? It is concluded, therefore, that it was not possible for Kṛṣṇa to do anything abominable.

Śukadeva Gosvāmī was an educated *brahmacārī,* and under the circumstances it was not possible for him to indulge in sex. This is strictly prohibited for *brahmacārīs,* and what to speak of a *brahmacārī* like Śukadeva Gosvāmī. But because the circumstances of the *rāsa* dance were very suspect, Mahārāja Parīkṣit inquired for clarification from Śukadeva Gosvāmī. Śukadeva Gosvāmī immediately replied that transgressions of religious principles by the supreme controller testify to His great power. For example, fire can consume any abominable thing; that is the manifestation of the supremacy of fire. Similarly, the sun can absorb water from a urinal or from stool, and the sun is not polluted; rather, due to the influence of the sunshine, the polluted, contaminated place becomes disinfected and sterilized.

One may also argue that since Kṛṣṇa is the supreme authority, His activities should be followed. In answer to this argument, Śukadeva Gosvāmī has very clearly said that the *īśvara*, or Supreme Controller, may sometimes violate His own instructions, but this is possible only for the Controller Himself, not for the followers.

A Māyāvādī philosopher may falsely claim to be God or Kṛṣṇa, but he cannot actually act like Kṛṣṇa. He can persuade his followers to falsely imitate the *rāsa* dance, but he is unable to lift Govardhana Hill. We have many experiences in the past of Māyāvādī rascals who delude their followers by posing themselves as Kṛṣṇa in order to enjoy *rāsa-līlā*. In many instances they were checked by the government, arrested, and punished. In Orissa, Ṭhākura Bhaktivinoda punished a so-called incarnation of Viṣṇu who was imitating the *rāsa-līlā* with young girls. There were many complaints against the so-called incarnation. At that time Bhaktivinoda Ṭhākura was a magistrate, and the government deputed him to deal with that rascal, and he punished him very severely. The *rāsa-līlā* dance cannot be imitated by anyone.

[*tābhir yutaḥ śramam apohitum aṅga-saṅga-*
ghṛṣṭa-srajaḥ sa kuca-kuṅkuma-rañjitāyāḥ
gandharva-pālibhir anudruta āviśad vāḥ
śrānto gajībhir ibha-rāḍ iva bhinna-setuḥ

(*Śrīmad-Bhāgavatam* 10.33.22)

Surrounded by so many she-elephants, along with black bees whose buzzing resembles the singing of the Gandharvas, a maddened elephant enters a river to bathe. Similarly, maddened in *prema*, Kṛṣṇa went with all His *gopī*-beloveds and entered the waters of Yamunā. As an intoxicated elephant smashes all the trees, flowers, and so on in its path, and enters the river with all his beloved she-elephants, Kṛṣṇa smashed, or in other words, transgressed, all *veda-dharma* (routine religious activities resulting in piety) and *loka-maryādā* (worldly morality) by sporting with the wives of other *gopas*.

Kṛṣṇa was wearing a garland of white *kunda* flowers (jasmine). Just as an intoxicated elephant smashes everything in its path, so after Kṛṣṇa's white garland was colored vermilion by the *kuṅkuma* powder on the breasts of the *gopīs*, it was crushed and strewn to pieces as He embraced them.

That garland was like a mediator. When two persons are quarrelling and a mediator is in the middle, the mediator gets smashed. Similarly, that garland was smashed and colored by the *gopīs' kuṅkuma*, as if bleeding.

That garland bore the scent of Kṛṣṇa's body and the *gopīs'* bodies, and also the scent of the *kunda* flowers themselves. So many fragrances mixed together, but at the same time, Kṛṣṇa's fragrance was perceived separately and Śrīmatī Rādhikā's separate fragrance was even sweeter than His. All the aromas were combined, and at the same time separate. Only persons with full knowledge were aware of all this; not others.

Kṛṣṇa realized the exalted transcendental experience of this pastime, the *gopīs* realized it, and the bees who hovered around Kṛṣṇa's garland to taste the honey of its fragrance also realized it. Therefore, wherever Kṛṣṇa would go, all the *gopīs* would go, and all the bees would go as well. In this way, Kṛṣṇa and the *gopīs* entered the Yamunā to play and splash water on each other.

Kṛṣṇa was performing His *nara-līlā*, or human-like pastimes. He is not a human being of this world, but He was playing like a human. Humans are not allowed to do as He did. Such activities are restricted in all the Vedas.

> If any mortal person breaks the rules and regulations of the Vedas, he is to be punished in hell, in court, by the police, and also by society. He will be punished by all.][4]

Śukadeva Gosvāmī warns that one should not even think of imitating it. He specifically mentions that if, out of foolishness, one tries to imitate Kṛṣṇa's *rāsa* dance, he will be killed, just like a person who wants to imitate Lord Śiva's drinking of an ocean of poison. Lord Śiva drank an ocean of poison and kept it within his throat. The poison made his throat turn blue, and therefore Lord Śiva is called Nīlakaṇṭha. But if any ordinary person tries to imitate Lord Śiva by drinking poison or smoking *gāñjā*, he is sure to be vanquished and will die within a very short time.

Lord Śrī Kṛṣṇa's dealings with the *gopīs* occurred under special circumstances. Most of the *gopīs* in their previous lives were great sages, expert in the study of the Vedas, and when Lord Kṛṣṇa appeared as Lord Rāmacandra they wanted to enjoy with Him. Lord Rāmacandra gave them the benediction that their desires would be fulfilled when He would appear as Kṛṣṇa. Therefore the desire of the *gopīs* to enjoy the appearance of Lord Kṛṣṇa was long cherished. So they approached goddess Kātyāyanī to have Kṛṣṇa as their husband.

Kṛṣṇa, the Supreme Personality of Godhead, was already present as the Supersoul within the bodies of the *gopīs* and their husbands. He is the guide of all living entities, as is confirmed in the *Kaṭha Upaniṣad*: *nityo nityānāṁ cetanaś cetanānām*. The Supersoul directs the individual soul to act, and the Supersoul is the actor and witness of all action. [...] Kṛṣṇa, the Supersoul of everyone, is already within the body of everyone; therefore if He sees someone or embraces someone there is no question of impropriety.

---

4 This insertion is an excerpt from a *darśana* with Śrīla Bhaktivedānta Nārāyaṇa Gosvāmī Mahārāja, spoken in November, 1993.

In the Second Canto of *Śrīmad-Bhāgavatam,* Mahārāja Parīkṣit also explains that the pastimes and activities of Lord Kṛṣṇa are medicine for the conditioned souls. If they simply hear about Kṛṣṇa, they become relieved of the material disease. They are addicted to material enjoyment and are accustomed to reading sex literature, but by hearing these transcendental pastimes of Kṛṣṇa with the *gopīs,* they will be relieved of material contamination.

Glossary

A

ācārya – spiritual preceptor; one who teaches by example. One who accepts the confidential meanings of the scriptures (*śāstra*) and engages others accordingly in *sad-ācāra*, or proper behavior, and who personally follows that *ācāra*, or behavior, himself, is described as *ācārya*.

akiñcana – one without material possessions; Kṛṣṇa and *kṛṣṇa-sevā* being one's sole possession.

anartha – *an-artha* means 'non-value;' unwanted desires, activities or habits that impede one's advancement in *bhakti*. In other words, everything that is against *bhakti*. These *anarthas* are of four types: (1) *duṣkṛtottha*, those arising from past sins; (2) *sukṛtottha*, those arising from previous pious activities; (3) *aparādhottha*, those arising from offenses; and (4) *bhakty-uttha*, those arising in relationship to *bhakti*.

anartha-nivṛtti – freedom from sinful activities; the elimination or clearing of all unwanted desires from the heart. This is the fourth stage in the development of the creeper of devotion, which occurs by the influence of *sādhu-saṅga* (association of pure devotees) and *bhajana-kriyā* (execution of the limbs of *bhakti*).

anubhāva – signs of ecstacy; see Endnote 1, at the end of Part 1.

anurāga – profound attachment; the stage of *prema* that is above *raga*, characterized by continuously renewed attachment for Śrī Kṛṣṇa.

āsakti – deep attachment. This refers to deep attachment for the Lord and His eternal associates. *Āsakti* occurs when ones liking for *bhajana* leads to a direct attachment for the person who is the object of that *bhajana*. This is the seventh stage in the development of the creeper of devotion, and it is awakened upon the maturing of one's taste for *bhajana*.

āśrama – (1) spiritual order; one of the four stages of life – student (*brahmacārī*), married (*gṛhastha*), retired (*vanaprastha*), or renounced (*sannyāsa*) – in which one carries out corresponding socio-religious duties in the system known as *varṇāśrama*. (2) a hermitage, usually in the association of others, which is established to facilitate spiritual practices.

aṣṭa-kālīya-līlā – the eternal pastimes which Śrī Kṛṣṇa performs with His associates in the eight periods of the day and night.

ātmā – the soul

B

bābājī – originally a term of respect which is given to *sādhus* (advanced devotees) and Vaiṣṇavas, particularly those who have given up all connection with household life. These days, the term is given loosely and often improperly to those who wear the dress of a *sādhu* but do not actually follow strict renunciation.

***bābājī-veśa* initiation** – (1) when the disciple reaches the stage of *bhāva-bhakti*, he naturally receives his *ekādaśa-bhāvas* (eleven sentiments of *gopī-bhāva*) from his spiritual master. However, in recent times this process has been perverted and, without consideration of qualification or disqualification, so-called *siddha-praṇālī* and an un-bona fide *bābājī-veśa* initiation with *mantras* is given even to neophytes, who are ignorant of *śāstra* and *siddhānta*; (2) the bona fide *bābājī-veśa* initiation is very similar to the *sannyāsa* initiation, in the sense that the *mantra* given by the spiritual master is the same. The difference is that to those who are mainly inclined to doing personal *bhajana*, the white garments of the *bābājī* order are given, whereas those who are also inclined to preaching receive the saffron colored garments of a *sannyāsī*.

bhāgavata-paramparā – the succession of bona fide *gurus* rooted in receiving and following transcendental instructions from their predecessors; see Endnote 5, at the end of Part 3.

bhajana – activities performed with the consciousness of being a servant of Śrī Kṛṣṇa (see *Garuḍa Purāṇa, Pūrvakhaṇḍa* 231.3, which explains that the verbal root *bhaj* is used specifically in the sense of *sevā*, or service); in a general sense, *bhajana* refers to the performance of spiritual practices, especially hearing, chanting and meditating upon Śrī Kṛṣṇa's name, form, qualities and pastimes.

bhajana-kriyā – engagement in devotional practices such as hearing and chanting. This is the third stage in the development of the creeper of devotion, and it occurs by the influence of *sādhu-saṅga*.

bhakta – a devotee; one who performs *bhakti*, or devotional service.

bhakti – loving devotional service to Śrī Kṛṣṇa. The word *bhakti* comes from the root *bhaj*, which means to serve; therefore the primary meaning of the word *bhakti* is to render service. The performance of activities which are meant exclusively for the pleasure of the Supreme Lord Śrī Kṛṣṇa, which are done in a favorable spirit saturated with love, which are devoid of all other desires, and which are not covered by *karma* (the pursuits of fruitive activity) and *jñāna* (the cultivation of knowledge aimed at merging one's existence into that of the Lord) is called *bhakti*.

bhāva – spiritual emotions, love or sentiments; the eighth stage (just before *prema*, tranāscendental love) in the development of the creeper of *bhakti*. *Bhāva* can also refer to one's *sthāyī-bhāva*, or one's permanent sentiment of love for Śrī Kṛṣṇa in one of five primary relationships: tranquility (*śānta*), servitude (*dāsya*), friendship (*sakhya*), parental affection (*vātsalya*), or conjugal love (*mādhurya*).

bhāva-bhakti – the initial stage of perfection in devotion. A stage of *bhakti* in which *śuddha-sattva*, the essence of the Lord's internal potency consisting of spiritual knowledge and bliss, is transmitted into the heart of the practicing devotee from the heart of the Lord's eternal associates. It is the first sprout of pure love of God (*prema*), and it is also known as *rati*.

D

daṇḍa – a stick carried by *sannyāsīs*, renunciates in the fourth stage of life according to the Vedic social system.

daṇḍavat -praṇāma – prostrated obeisances; literally, falling like a *daṇḍa* (stick) to offer *praṇāma* (obeisances).

darśana – a direct vision of, or an audience with, someone

dharma – constitutional nature; principles of religious conduct; religiosity; righteous prescription.

dhotī – a single, long piece of cloth, traditionally worn by Indian men to cover the lower half of the body.

dīkṣā – initiation from a spiritual master; in the *Bhakti-sandarbha* (*Anuccheda* 283) Śrīla Jīva Gosvāmī has defined *dīkṣā* as follows: "Learned exponents of the Absolute Truth declare that the process by which the spiritual master imparts divine knowledge (*divya-jñāna*) to the disciple and eradicates all sins is known as *dīkṣā*." He then explains *divya- jñāna* as "the transcendental knowledge of the Lord's form and one's specific relationship with the Lord contained within a *mantra*." This means that at the time of initiation, the *guru* gives the disciple a *mantra* which, in course of time, reveals the particular form of the Lord who is the object of one's worship and the disciple's specific relationship with the Lord in one of the relationships of *dāsya*, *sakhya*, *vātsalya* or *mādhurya*.

ḍor-kaupīna – the two cloths that signify one's renunciation from material sense gratification.

E

ekādaśa-bhāva – the eleven aspects of *gopī-bhāva*; the eleven transcendental *bhāvas*, or sentiments, received upon attaining one's *siddha-svarūpa*; see '*Siddha-deha, Our Spiritual Body*' in Part 1 (p 5–6).

Ekādaśī – a fast, observed on the eleventh day of the lunar fortnight, from grains and beans (minimum) so that the *bhakta,* devotee, can totally immerse himself in activities of pure *bhakti*; *bhakti-jananī* (the mother of *bhakti*). If one follows one's *vrata* (vow) devotionally on this day, She, as mother, will allow pure *bhakti* to take birth within one's heart. *Śuddha* Ekādaśī means that the whole eleventh day of the moon elapses during the period between one sunrise and the next. *Viddha* Ekādaśī means that the eleventh day of the moon begins on one solar day (sunrise to sunrise) and finishes on the next solar day, that is, after sunrise on the next day. In case of *Viddha* Ekādaśī, the observances are made on the Dvādaśī, that is, the twelfth day of the moon.

G

Gauḍīya Vaiṣṇavism – the school of Vaiṣṇavism that follows in the line of Śrī Caitanya Mahāprabhu, headed by Śrīla Rūpa, Śrīla Raghunātha and other Gosvāmīs.

gopī – one of the young cowherd maidens of Vraja, headed by Śrīmatī Rādhikā, who serve Kṛṣṇa in a mood of amorous love; an elderly associate of Mother Yaśodā, who serves Kṛṣṇa in a mood of parental affection.

gṛhastha – the word *stha* means 'to reside.' The word *gṛha* means 'house,' and also refers to the family members who inhabit a house; as a verb, it means 'to grasp,' 'take on,' or 'accept.' The second *āśrama*, or stage of life, in the *varṇāśrama* system; a householder; one who is in family life.

guru, gurudeva – spiritual master.

H

harināma – the chanting of Śrī Kṛṣṇa's holy names. Unless accompanied by the word *saṅkīrtana*, it usually refers to the practice of chanting the Hare Kṛṣṇa *mahā-mantra* softly to oneself on a strand of *tulasī* beads.

J

jagad-guru – the spiritual master of the entire Universe; one who is qualified to act as a spiritual master to anyone in the entire world.

Janmāṣṭamī – the appearance day of Lord Śrī Kṛṣṇa, which occurs on the eighth day of the dark lunar fortnight of the month of Bhādra (August-September).

jīva – the living entity who, in the conditioned stage of material existence, assumes a material body in any of the innumerable species of life.

K

kīrtana – one of the nine most important limbs of *bhakti*, consisting of either: (1) congregational singing of Śrī Kṛṣṇa's holy names, usually accompanied by music; (2) loud individual chanting of the holy name; or (3) oral descriptions of the glories of Śrī Kṛṣṇa's names, forms, qualities, associates and pastimes.

kṛṣṇa-prema – pure love for Śrī Kṛṣṇa.

kuñja – a secluded forest grove; a natural, shady retreat with a roof and walls formed by trees, vines, creepers and other climbing plants.

L

līlā – the divine and astonishing pastimes of Śrī Kṛṣṇa and His eternal associates.

M

mādana – the highest form of *adhirūḍha-mahābhava*, found only in Śrīmatī Rādhikā.

madhura-rasa*, or *mādhurya-rasa – amorous love; one of the five primary relationships with Kṛṣṇa established in the stage of *bhāva* and *prema*; love or attachment toward Kṛṣṇa which is expressed in the mood of a lover. This mood is eternally present in the *gopīs* of Vraja.

mahā-bhāgavata – a pure devotee of the Lord in the highest stage of devotional life, who is expert in Vedic literature, has full faith in Śrī Kṛṣṇa, and can deliver the whole world.

mahābhāva – the highest, unexcelled stage of *prema.*

māna – vexation in love; an intensified stage of *prema.*

mānasa-sevā, or ***mānasī-sevā*** – service rendered within the mind to one's worshipable Deity.

mañjarī – a maidservant of Śrīmatī Rādhikā.

mañjarī-bhāva – the mood of Śrīmatī Rādhikā's maidservants.

mantra – (*man* = mind; *tra* = deliverance) a spiritual sound vibration that delivers the mind from its material conditioning and illusion when repeated over and over; a Vedic hymn, prayer or chant.

mātājī – literally: 'mother;' in the context of this book it refers to (often widow) ladies who live in the *āśramas* of *sahajiyā-bābājīs*, and in the name of spiritual practice engage in paramour relationships with those *bābājīs*.

māyā – the Lord's deluding potency; illusion, or illusory energy; that which is not; the Lord's external potency, which influences the living entities to accept the false egoism of being independent enjoyers of this material world. Also called *mahāmāyā* or *māyā-śakti.*

Māyāvāda – the doctrine of illusion; a theory advocated by the impersonalist followers of Śaṅkarācārya which holds that the Lord's form, this material world, and the individual existence of the living entities, are *māyā,* or false. This philosophy accepts the authority of Vedic texts, but interprets them in such a way as to advance an impersonal conception of the Absolute and deny the personal feature of Godhead. It is known as covered Buddhism, since Buddhism is overtly atheistic.

mohana – *adhirūḍha-mahābhava,* the highest form of conjugal love, is divided into two cateogories: in meeting, a state called *mādana* manifests, yet when the lover and beloved become separated, *mohana,* or bewilderment, occurs. As an effect of this helpless condition of separation, one becomes stunned and all the bodily symptoms of transcendental ecstasy (*sāttvika-bhāvas*) manifest.

N

nikuñja – a secluded grove wherein Śrī Kṛṣṇa and the *gopīs* perform their confidential amorous pastimes.

niṣkiñcana – free from all material possessions, entirely destitute; a renunciate.

niṣṭhā – (1) firm faith which results in steadiness in one's devotional practices. This is the fourth stage in the development of the devotional creeper. It occurs after the elimination of a significant portion of one's *anarthas.*

P

pāñcarātrika-paramparā – the disciplic line based on receiving formal *mantras*; see Endnote 5, at the end of Part 3.

pālya-dāsī – a maidservant of Śrīmatī Rādhikā. The word *pālya* means to be nourished, cared for, and protected, and the word *dāsī* means a female servant. Thus the *pālya-dāsīs* are the maidservants under the affectionate care of Śrīmatī Rādhikā.

parakīya-bhāva – paramour love; an amorous relationship outside of marriage.

paramahaṁsa – a topmost, God-realized, swan-like devotee of the Lord.

paramparā – disciplic succession.

praṇāma – literally: 'bowing to the ground;' an offering of respect and dedication. One should especially offer *praṇāma* before the Deity of the Lord, *śrī guru*, *tridaṇḍī-sannyāsīs*, and devotees whose hearts are free from the propensity to criticize others.

praṇaya – a stage of *prema* above *māna*, characterized by unrestrained intimacy, known as *viśrambha*.

prema – divine, transcendental love; the deep longing to satisfy the senses of Śrī Kṛṣṇa who, being more dear to one than one's own soul, is the object of intense possessiveness.

R

rāga – deep attachment for the object of one's affection; the stage of *prema* above *praṇaya*.

rāgānuga, rāgānuga-bhakti – *bhakti* that follows in the wake of Śrī Kṛṣṇa's eternal associates of Vraja, whose hearts are permeated with *rāga*, which is an unquenchable loving thirst for Kṛṣṇa that gives rise to spontaneous and intense absorption.

rāgātmika – one in whose heart a deep, spontaneous desire to love and serve Śrī Kṛṣṇa exists naturally and eternally. This specifically refers to the eternal residents of Vraja.

rasa – the spiritual transformation of the heart which takes place when the perfectional state of love for Śrī Kṛṣṇa, known as *rati*, is converted into 'liquid' emotions by combining various types of transcendental ecstasies; taste, flavor.

rasika – one who is expert at relishing *rasa*.

rati – attachment, fondness for; a stage in the development of *bhakti* which is synonymous with *bhāva*; also see *bhāva*.

ruci – taste; this is the sixth stage in the development of the creeper of devotion, which develops after one has acquired steadiness in *bhajana*. At this stage, with the awakening of actual taste, one's attraction to spiritual matters such as hearing, chanting, and other devotional practices exceeds one's attraction to any type of material activity.

rūpānuga, rūpānuga-bhakti – a follower of Śrīla Rūpa Gosvāmī; *bhakti* which follows the particular devotional sentiment cherished within the heart of Śrī Rūpa Mañjarī.

S

sad-guru – a bona fide spiritual master; spiritual preceptor who follows *sat* (the pure path of the *sādhus* as described within scripture and as delivered through *paramparā*).

sādhaka – practitioner; one who performs *sādhana*, a spiritual discipline, to achieve the specific goal of *bhāva-bhakti*.

sādhana – the method one adopts in order to obtain a specific goal (*sādhya*) is called *sādhana*. Without *sādhana* one cannot obtain *sādhya*, the goal of one's practice. There are many different types of *sādhana* corresponding to various goals. Those who desire material enjoyment adopt the path of *karma* as their *sādhana*. Those who desire liberation adopt the path of *jñāna* as their *sādhana*. Those who aspire for the eternal loving service of Śrī Kṛṣṇa adopt the path of *bhakti* as their *sādhana*. The *sādhana* of *bhakti* refers to spiritual practices such as hearing, chanting and so on.

sādhu – a highly-realized soul who knows life's aim (*sādhya*), who is himself practising *sādhana* (the process to attain *sādhya*), and who can engage others in *sādhana*; (in a general sense) a saintly person or devotee.

sādhu-saṅga – the association of highly advanced devotees; it is the second stage in the development of the creeper of devotion and the most important factor for advancement in *bhakti*.

sahajiyā – the word *sahaja* comes from *saha-ja*, that is, that which arises along with the *ātmā*. For the pure *ātmā*, transcendental service to Kṛṣṇa is *sahaja*, or natural, because it is intrinsic to the *jīvātmā's* constitution. In the context of this book however, the word *sahajiyā* is used for a specific group of people, the *prākṛta-sahajiyās*, who understand the transcendental pastimes (*aprākṛta-līlā*) of the transcendental Supreme Lord to be *prākṛta*, or mundane, like the affairs of ordinary men and women, and who think that the *aprākṛta-tattva* (transcendental truth) is attained by material practices. They consider the stages of advanced devotion to be easily and cheaply achieved, and thus sometimes imitate the external symptoms of spiritual ecstasy associated with those stages.

sakhī – a female friend, companion, or attendant; a *gopī* friend.

sampradāya – a particular school of religious teaching; an established doctrine, transmitted from one teacher to another; a line of disciplic succession.

sannyāsa – (1) completely giving up the results of one's activities. (2) the fourth *āśrama,* or stage of life, in the *varṇāśrama* system.There are four stages of *sannyāsa*: *kūṭīcaka* – one who resides in a *kūṭīr* (hut) and accepts alms from a family or *āśrama* till his *sādhana* reaches maturity; *bahūdaka* – then he travels on pilgrimage and bathes in *bahu* (many) *udakas* (waters), practicing detachment through dependence on Bhagavān; *parivrājak* – then, when *divya-jñāna*, transcendental knowledge, arises in his heart, he preaches his realizations to everyone in every village; *paramahaṁsa* – by full absorption in *kṛṣṇa-kathā, kṛṣṇa-tattva,* and *kṛṣṇa-kīrtana,* he becomes fully mature and the *haṁsa* (swan) of his mind always dives and surfaces in Śrī Śrī Rādhā-Kṛṣṇa's ever new pastimes.

śāstra – Vedic scripture; derived from the Sanskrit verbal root *śās* (to govern, command). Thus, *śāstric* injunctions are authoritative and accepted as Absolute Truth.

sāttvika-bhāva – ecstatic transformation; see Endnote 1, at the end of Part 1.

sevā – service, reverence, devotion to.

siddha-deha – one's perfected spiritual identity or spiritual body, which is beyond this gross and subtle material body, and which is fit to serve Śrī Śrī Rādhā and Kṛṣṇa.

siddhānta – conclusive truth; authoritative principle of scripture.

siddha-praṇālī – the process, or system, that gives spiritual perfection.

śikhā – tuft of hair at the back of the head, worn by devotees as a sign of devotion; in Vedic culture a little boy's head is shaved at the age of one, three, or five years, and only a *śikhā* (or *choti*) remains. As the hair grows back again, the *śikhā* naturally also grows and remains longer than the rest of the hair.

śikṣā – instructions received from a teacher; as one of the limbs of *bhakti,* this specifically refers to instructions received from a *guru* about *bhakti.*

sneha – deep affection; the stage of *prema-bhakti* above the stage of *prema*, characterized by deep affection that causes the heart to melt.

śloka – a Sanskrit verse.

śraddhā – initial faith; faith in the statements of *guru, sādhu* and scriptures. *Śraddhā* is awakened when one has accumulated devotional pious activities over many births, or by the association and mercy of a transcendental person who has dedicated his life to the service of Lord Kṛṣṇa. It is the first stage in the development of the creeper of devotion.

sthāyībhāva – permanent emotion; see Endnote 1, at the end of Part 1.

śuddha – pure.

svakīya-bhāva – wedded conjugal love; the mood of devotion wherein the devotee considers the Lord to be her lawfully wedded husband.

svarūpa – the eternal nature and identity of the self; one's transcendental form. It can also refer to the transcendental forms of Śrī Śrī Rādhā and Kṛṣṇa.

svarūpa-śakti – the Lord's internal potency; see Endnote 3, at the end of Part 1.

T

tattva – truth, reality, philosophical principle; the essence or substance of anything.

tridaṇḍi – a staff which is carried by the Vaiṣṇava *sannyāsīs*. It consists of three rods, symbolising engagement of body, mind, and words in the service of the Lord. These three rods may also signify the eternal existence of the servitor (the *bhakta*), the object of service (Bhagavān), and service, thus distinguishing Vaiṣṇava *sannyāsa* from the *māyāvāda eka-daṇḍa* ('one rod') *sannyāsa*.

tulasi – the sacred plant whose leaves and blossoms are used by Vaiṣṇavas in the worship of Śrī Kṛṣṇa; the wood is also used for making chanting beads and neck beads; a partial expansion of Vṛndā-devī.

V

vaidhī-bhakti – devotion prompted by the regulations of the scriptures. When *sādhana-bhakti* is not inspired by intense longing, but is instigated by the discipline of scriptures, it is called *vaidhī-bhakti*.

Vaiṣṇava – literally means 'one whose nature is of Viṣṇu,' in other words, one in whose heart and mind only Viṣṇu (or Kṛṣṇa) resides; a devotee of Śrī Kṛṣṇa or Viṣṇu.

varṇāśrama-dharma – *varṇa* means 'social order' and *āśrama* means 'a place of *āśraya* (spiritual shelter);' a shelter for mankind ensuring both material and spiritual advancement; the Vedic system for the organization of civilized society, which divides society into four *varṇas,* or orders, of *brāhmaṇa* (priest or teacher), *kṣatriya* (warrior or statesman), *vaiśya* (agriculturalist, merchant, or businessman), *śūdra (laborer),* and the four *āśramas* (stages of life) of *brahmācārya* (unmarried student life), *gṛhastha* (family life), *vānaprastha* (retirement from family responsibilities), and *sannyāsa* (the renounced ascetic life).

veśa – one's dress, or garments.

vibhāva – the causes for tasting *bhakti-rasa*; see Endnote 1, at the end of Part 1.

Vraja, Vṛndāvana – the eighty-four square-mile track of land where Śrī Kṛṣṇa enacted His childhood and youthful pastimes with His cowherd friends, girl-friends, parents, and well-wishers.

vyabhicāri-bhāva – transitory ecstacies; see Endnote 1, at the end of Part 1.

English titles published by
Śrī Śrīmad Bhaktivedānta Nārāyaṇa Gosvāmī Mahārāja

• Arcana-dīpikā • Beyond Nīrvāṇa • Bhagavad-gītā • Bhajana-rahasya • Bhakti-rasāmṛta-sindu-bindu • Bhakti-rasāyana •Bhakti-tattva-viveka • Brahma-saṁhitā • Bṛhad-bhāgavatāmṛta (Vol. 2.1) • Caitanya Mahāprabhu – The Original Form of Godhead • Camatkāra-candrikā • Dāmodara-līlā-mādhurī • Dāmodarāṣṭakam • Essence of All Advice • Essence of Bhagavad-gītā • Fearless Prince • Five Essential Essay •Gauḍīya Gīti-guccha • Discerning the True Sentiments of the Soul • Gaura-vāṇī Pracāriṇe • Gift of Śrī Caitanya Mahāprabhu • Gīta-govinda • Going Beyond Vaikuṇṭha • Gopī-gīta • Guru-devatātmā • Harināma Mahā-mantra • Harmony • Hidden Path of Devotion • Impressions of Bhakti • Jaiva-dharma • Journey of the Soul • Letters from America • Maharṣi Durvāsā and Śrī Durvāsā-āśrama • Manaḥ-śikṣā • My Śikṣā-guru and Priya-bandhu • Navadvīpa-dhāma-māhātmya • Navadvīpa-dhāma • Nectar of Govinda-līlā • Origin of Ratha-yātrā • Our Eternal Nature • Pinnacle of Devotion • Prabandhāvalī • Prema-sampuṭa • Rādhā-kṛṣṇa-gaṇoddeśa-dīpikā • Rāya Rāmānanda Saṁvāda • Saṅkalpa-kalpadrumaḥ • Secrets of the Undiscovered Self •Secret Truths of the Bhāgavatam • Śikṣāṣṭaka • Śiva-tattva • Ślokāmṛtam • Ślokāmṛtam-bindu • Śrī Śrīmad Bhakti Prajñāna Keśava Gosvāmī – His Life and Teachings • The Butter Thief • Their Lasting Relation • To Be Controlled by Love • True Conception of Guru-tattva • Ujjvala-nīlamaṇi-kiraṇa • Upadeśāmṛta • Utkalikā-vallarī • Vaiṣṇava-siddhānta-mālā • Veṇu-gīta • Vraja-maṇḍala Parikramā • Walking with a Saint (2007, 2008, 2009) • Way of Love • Rays of The Harmonist (periodical)

FOR MORE INFORMATION

www.purebhakti.com

for news, updates, and free downloads of books, lectures, and *bhajanas*

www.purebhakti.tv

to watch and hear, or to download classes online

www.harikatha.com

to receive, by email, the lectures and videos of Śrīla Bhaktivedānta Nārāyaṇa Gosvāmī Mahārāja on his world tours

If you are interested to know more about the books, lectures, audios, videos, teachings, and international society of Śrī Śrīmad Bhaktivedānta Nārāyaṇa Gosvāmī Mahārāja, please contact us at

connectwithussoon@gmail.com

GVP WEBSITES

www.bhaktistore.com

www.mygvp.com

www.gvpbookdistribution.com

YOUR COMMENTS AND FEEDBACK

We humbly invite our readers to submit any errors they may find at

www.purebhakti.com/gvp

WORLDWIDE CENTRES & CONTACTS

WORLD WIDE

www.purebhakti.com/contact-us/centers-mainmenu-60.html

INDIA

Mathura: *Shri Kesavaji Gaudiya Matha* – Jawahar Hata, U.P. 281001 (Opp. Dist. Hospital), Email: mathuramath@gmail.com • **New Delhi**: Shri Ramana-vihari Gaudiya Matha – Block B-3, Janakpuri, New Delhi 110058 (Near musical fountain park), Tel: 9810192540; *Karol Bagh Centre*: Rohini-nandana dasa, 9A/39 Channa Market, WEA, Karol Bagh, Tel: 9810398406, 9810636370, Email: purebhakti.kb@gmail.com • **Vrindavan**: *Shri Rupa-Sanatana Gaudiya Matha* – Dan Gali, U.P. Tel: 09760952435; Gopinath Bhavan – Parikrama Marga (next to Imli-tala), Seva Kunja, Vrindavan 281121, U.P., Email: vasantidasi@gmail.com • **Puri**: *Jayasri Damodar Gaudiya Matha* – Sea Palace, Chakratirtha Road. Tel: 06752-227617 • **Bangalore**: *Shri Madana Mohan Gaudiya Matha* – 245/1 29th Cross, Kaggadasa pura Balaji layout, Bangalore-93, Tel: 089044277754, Email: giridharidas@gmail.com • **Faridabad**: *Shri Radha Madhava Gaudiya Math* – 293, Sector-14, Hariyana, Tel: 09911283869 • **Navadvipa**: *Shri Shri Kesavaji Gaudiya Math* – Kolerdanga Lane, Nadiya, Bengal, Tel: 09153125442

AUSTRALIA

Garden Ashram – Akhileshvari dasi, Tel: 612 66795916, Email: akhileshvari.dasi@gmail.com • *Shri Gaura Narayana Gaudiya Matha*, Brisbane, Queensland, Tel: +61 403 993 746, Email: bhaktibrisbane2010@gmail.com

CHINA / HONG KONG

15A, Hillview Court, 30 Hillwood Road, Tsim Sha Tsui, Kowloon, Tel: +85223774603

UNITED KINGDOM & IRELAND

Birmingham: *Shri Gour Govinda Gaudiya Math* – 9 Clarence Road, Handsworth, Birmingham, B21 0ED, UK, Tel: (44) 121551-7729, Email: bvashram108@gmail.com • **London**: *Ganga-mata Gaudiya Matha* – Email: gangamatajis@yahoo.co.uk • **Galway**: *Family Centre* – Tel: 353 85-1548200, Email: jagannathchild@gmail.com

USA

Gaudiya Vedanta Publications Offices – Tel: (800) 681-3040 ext. 108, Email: orders@bhaktiprojects.org • **Houston**: *Preaching Center* – Tel: (1) 713-984 8334, Email: byshouston@gmail.com